The Pocket Guide to Professional Responsibility

Fourth Edition

Arthur Garwin

Center for Professional Responsibility • American Bar Association

Cover design by Catherine Zaccarine.

The materials contained herein represent the opinions of the authors and/or the editors and should not be construed to be the action of either the American Bar Association or the Center for Professional Responsibility unless adopted pursuant to the bylaws of the Association.

Nothing contained in this book is to be considered as the rendering of legal advice, either generally or in connection with any specific issue or case. Nor do these materials purport to explain or interpret any specific bond or policy, or any provisions thereof, issued by any particular insurance company, or to render insurance or other professional advice. Readers are responsible for obtaining advice from their own lawyer or other professional. This book and any forms and agreements herein are intended for educational and informational purposes only.

© 2015 American Bar Association. All rights reserved.

No part of this publication may be reproduced, stored in a retrieval system, or transmitted in any form or by any means, electronic, mechanical, photocopying, recording, or otherwise, without the prior written permission of the publisher. For permission contact the ABA Copyrights & Contracts Department, copyright@americanbar.org or via fax at 312-988-6030, or complete the online form at http://www.americanbar.org/utility/reprint.html.

21 20 19 18   5 4 3 2

Library of Congress Cataloging-in-Publication Data

Garwin, Arthur, 1949– editor
  The paralegal's guide to professional responsibility / By Arthur H. Garwin.—Fourth edition.
      pages cm
  Includes bibliographical references and index.
  ISBN 978-1-63425-201-0 (print : alk. paper)
  1. Legal ethics—United States. 2. Legal assistants—United States—Handbooks, manuals, etc. I. Title.
  KF306.G37 2015
  174'.30973—dc23
                                                                    2015026275

Discounts are available for books ordered in bulk. Special consideration is given to state bars, CLE programs, and other bar-related organizations. Inquire at ABA Publishing, Book Publishing, American Bar Association, 321 N. Clark Street, Chicago, Illinois 60654-7598.

www.ShopABA.org

ABA CENTER FOR PROFESSIONAL RESPONSIBILITY PUBLICATIONS BOARD

John Sahl, *Chair*
Akron, Ohio

Susan Saab Fortney
Hempstead, New York

Arthur F. Greenbaum
Columbus, Ohio

Andrew M. Perlman
Boston, Massachusetts

Natasha T. Martin
Seattle, WA

Maritza L. Reyes
Orlando, FL

Ronald D. Rotunda
Orange, California

Mark K. Tuft
San Francisco, California

Contents

Foreword vii

Acknowledgments ix

Introduction xi

Chapter One
The Role of the Paralegal 1

Chapter Two
The Legal Services Delivery Team 11

Chapter Three
The Law of Professional Responsibility 25

Chapter Four
Unauthorized Practice of Law 37

Chapter Five
Competence and Diligence 49

Chapter Six
Confidentiality 63

Chapter Seven
Conflicts of Interest 81

Chapter Eight
Communications 97

Chapter Nine
Information about Legal Services 105

Chapter Ten
Legal Fees and Employee Compensation   119

Chapter Eleven
Client Funds and Property   129

Appendix A
NALA Code of Ethics and Professional Responsibility   145

Appendix B
NFPA Model Code of Ethics and Professional Responsibility
and Guidelines for Enforcement   149

Appendix C
ABA Model Guidelines for the Utilization of Paralegal Services 157

Appendix D
AAfPE Core Competencies for Paralegal Programs   159

Appendix E
Legal Research Resources   169

Appendix F
Model Rules for Client Trust Account Records   179

Appendix G
Recap of Selected ABA Model Rules of Professional Conduct   187

Appendix H
Glossary   193

Index   199

.... Foreword

▶ This handbook may be used as a desk reference, a companion piece for each jurisdiction's lawyer ethics rules, a basic text for a paralegal ethics class, assigned reading as part of a paralegal's orientation to a law firm or other paralegal employer, or as part of an in-house training program in legal ethics.

Chapter 1 creates the setting for a discussion of legal ethics and professional conduct by addressing these questions: What is the professional role of the paralegal in relation to clients, lawyers, the legal system, and the public? What does professionalism mean for a paralegal?

Chapter 2 answers the following questions: Who created regulations for the conduct of service providers? What is the relative authority of various rules and opinions governing the conduct of legal service providers? What other substantive areas of law govern the professional conduct of lawyers and paralegals? How does the law of agency operate in relationships between lawyers, paralegals, and clients? What are the consequences of violating professional conduct rules?

Chapters 3 through 11 examine rules, guidelines, and legal developments in areas of the law of professional responsibility that particularly impact the paralegal. Each chapter contains a bulleted summary of important concepts from the text.

The book concludes with a glossary of terms and several appendices containing requirements, rules, codes, and guidelines of use to the paralegal.

♦ A Note of Caution

This book has been developed as a tool for paralegals throughout the country. Based on the ABA Model Rules for Professional Conduct, it offers general guidance that can be adapted in any jurisdiction. Since specific ethics rules differ from jurisdiction to jurisdiction, it is essential that each reader consult his or her jurisdiction's rules of professional conduct.

.... *Acknowledgments*

▶ In the six years between the publication of the first edition of *The Legal Assistant's Practical Guide to Professional Responsibility* and the second edition, the ABA Model Rules of Professional Conduct were significantly amended as a result of the work of the Commission on Evaluation of the Rules of Professional Conduct (Ethics 2000 Commission), the Commission on Multijurisdictional Practice, the Task Force on Corporate Responsibility, and the Standing Committee on Ethics and Professional Responsibility.

In the seven years between the publication of the second and third editions (retitled *The Paralegal's Guide to Professional Responsibility*), several more amendments to the Model Rules were adopted, including, most importantly for the purposes of this book, changes to the rule regarding imputation of conflicts of interest.

The completion of the work of the Commission on Ethics 20/20 led to the production of this fourth edition, which encompasses the changes made by that commission, along with updates to case references and other resources.

The Center for Professional Responsibility thanks West Publishing for its generous gift of the West Professional

Responsibility Law Library, the resource for much of the research reflected in this work.

This edition, and the three that preceded it, would not have been possible without Jeanne P. Gray, who, for 30 years, provided unparalleled leadership and vision for the Center for Professional Responsibility.

Arthur H. Garwin, Director
Center for Professional Responsibility

Introduction

▸ With the steady growth of the paralegal profession, paralegals have become an integral part of modern law practice. As valued members of the legal service delivery team, paralegals must know and understand the legal profession's rules for dealing with lawyers, clients, judges, coworkers, and other parties.

The ABA Center for Professional Responsibility has developed this guide to provide a practical reference on the basics of professional conduct. This handbook contains explanations of the law of professional responsibility as it affects paralegals, tools for identifying and resolving ethical problems, and practical tips to use in everyday practice.

This handbook was prepared to educate paralegals, secretaries, and other employees of law firms, corporations, and law-related organizations about ethical standards and to encourage the professional conduct of those employees. It is intended to be used by paralegals or those involved in training programs.

Legal ethics is becoming increasingly complex for lawyers and paralegals alike. With greater accountability to clients, increased mobility for all law firm personnel, and a growing demand to improve the image of the legal profession, it is essential to keep abreast of current developments in ethics and to adhere to professional standards.

A breach of legal ethics can seriously damage a law firm's reputation and profitability, causing client dissatisfaction and possibly triggering legal consequences such as professional liability claims or disciplinary actions. An ounce of prevention, in the form of ethics education, is worth a pound of cure after an ethical breach. Those using this book should consult with their supervising lawyer as to any questions they may have about the issues presented.

Professional responsibility is a matter of paramount importance for everyone employed in the legal profession. We hope this handbook will be a useful resource for addressing these issues. For other publications from the Center for Professional Responsibility, see http://www.americanbar.org/groups/professional_responsibility/publications.html. For links to legal ethics resources outside the ABA, see http://www.americanbar.org/groups/professional_responsibility/resources/links_of_interest.html.

Chapter ONE

The Role of the Paralegal

♦ THE LAWYER-PARALEGAL RELATIONSHIP

Paralegals today perform many tasks that once were performed only by lawyers, such as preparing, filing, or producing documents. Law firms have for many years realized that their practices can be more cost efficient by hiring paralegals instead of lawyers to do these and other tasks. What was true over 20 years ago is still true today:

- Under present market conditions, clients are no longer willing to have all the work performed at lawyers' rates. Associate rates that once provided a solution to the high cost of legal work now contribute to the problem. Because of this, the legal assistant profession has become one of the fastest growing in the nation. Lawyers are beginning to recognize that they will be able to produce a greater volume of legal work if they shift a larger portion of work to nonlawyers.[1]

Paralegals can enhance profitability for law firms by performing a variety of work that lawyers would otherwise do, thereby reducing costs for clients (because paralegals' services are billed at lower rates) and increasing access to the legal system for individuals who might not otherwise be able to afford legal services.

The paralegal acts as an agent of the lawyer in regard to interaction with clients and others. As such, the paralegal owes the lawyer certain duties. Subsequent chapters will discuss these duties more fully in the context of the paralegal's function, but the general duties of an agent include the diligent and competent performance of tasks within the authority given by the principal and the avoidance of conflicts of interest. Maintaining confidentiality and communicating effectively would fall under these broad categories.

As lawyers are themselves agents (of their clients), they are subject to the same general duties. Lawyers' duties, which have been formalized into specific bodies of rules, are introduced in Chapter 2 and discussed throughout this book. Although these rules apply to lawyers and not to paralegals, paralegals as agents acting on behalf of their employers must help ensure that the rules are not violated. Model Rule of Professional Conduct 8.4 states, moreover, that "[i]t is professional misconduct for a lawyer to violate or attempt to violate the Rules of Professional Conduct . . . through the acts of another."

Consequences of rule violations usually fall upon the lawyer as the principal in the relationship, with deleterious effects on the firm and on the legal profession. However, paralegals can be held directly responsible for the unauthorized practice of law and other actions as described in later chapters.

The agency relationship between lawyer and paralegal, then, requires first and foremost that the paralegal understand the rules of conduct governing legal practice in the state where the lawyer is located. Next, the paralegal must refrain from any action that would cause a violation of the rules and mention any violation likely to occur as a result of lawyer or other staff actions.[2]

Thus, the relationship between lawyer and paralegal is one of shared goals and mutual responsibility. Working together, they can efficiently provide high-quality services. As members of a team, they owe certain obligations to one another. The lawyer must delegate, supervise, and assume ultimate responsibility for the paralegal's work. The paralegal should perform tasks competently, refrain from giving legal advice or otherwise engaging in the unauthorized practice of law, and keep the lawyer informed of progress on assignments.

The role of paralegals continues to change and expand. The work performed by paralegals is varied and complex and includes both routine tasks and more substantive tasks performed under the supervision of lawyers.

The principal employers of paralegals in the private sector are law firms. Other employers include insurance companies, estate and trust departments of financial institutions, real estate firms, title insurance companies, and corporate law departments, as well as nonprofit organizations such as unions, professional and trade associations, charitable organizations, and consumer and advocacy groups. Public-sector employers include courts, legal services programs, the military, and state and local government offices, such as those of public defenders and prosecutors. The largest employer of paralegals outside the private sector is the federal government.

◆ WHO ARE PARALEGALS?

Paralegals are a diverse group in terms of educational background. Some enter the field directly after high school and are trained on the job. Others advance to the paralegal ranks from clerical or secretarial backgrounds. Still others choose to obtain a paralegal certificate or a degree before beginning their careers. Many career changers are entering the field as well and securing postbaccalaureate credentials.

Paralegals in the United States are not licensed; jurisdictions do not impose requirements, such as an examination or a character and fitness evaluation, before individuals may undertake paralegal responsibilities. Some states, however, have instituted voluntary registration or certification programs for paralegals.[3]

In addition, some legal professional associations have recommended certain academic criteria they think are essential for entry into the field.

The National Association for Legal Assistants (NALA) and the National Federation of Paralegal Associations (NFPA), the two largest national paralegal associations, have adopted definitions of the terms "paralegal" and "legal assistant" that generally follow the one developed in 1997 by the ABA Standing Committee on Legal Assistants (now the Standing Committee on Paralegals):

> A legal assistant or paralegal is a person, qualified by education, training, or work experience, who is employed or retained by a lawyer, law office, corporation, governmental agency or other entity and who performs specifically delegated substantive legal work for which a lawyer is responsible.[4]

Further acknowledgment that paralegals are capable of carrying out many tasks that would otherwise be performed by a lawyer, and billed at a higher rate, came in *Missouri v. Jenkins*, a school desegregation case in which the U.S. Supreme Court allowed a separate compensation award for paralegals, law clerks, and recent law school graduates.[5] The Court there delineated the substantive duties paralegals perform:

> It has frequently been recognized in the lower courts that legal assistants are capable of carrying out many tasks, under the supervision of an attorney, that might otherwise be performed by a lawyer and billed at a higher rate. Such work might include, for example, factual investigation, including locating and interviewing witnesses; assistance with depositions, interrogatories, and document production; compilation of statistical and financial data; checking legal citations; and drafting correspondence. Much such work lies in a gray area of tasks that might appropriately be performed either by an attorney or a legal assistant.[6]

As paralegals acquire greater experience and in some instances develop specialized expertise in different areas of practice, they grow increasingly more competent in performing tasks that have traditionally been performed by lawyers. Experienced paralegals are often given progressively more responsibility and subjected to less direct supervision as they gain knowledge and skills. But, because the paralegal is the agent of the lawyer, who is ultimately responsible for all of the paralegal's actions, this increased responsibility includes an obligation to understand and uphold the same high ethical standards to which the lawyer is subject.

The Role of the Paralegal

▶ GROWTH OF THE PARALEGAL PROFESSION

While lawyers have employed legal secretaries or assistants for generations, it has only been since the 1960s that a clearly identifiable paralegal profession has emerged.[7] The rising cost of legal services threatened to exclude low-income and middle-income Americans from access to legal services, and local bar groups searched for ways to make legal services affordable while still protecting the public. The solution was the creation of a profession of specially trained paralegals.

Initially, the only training available to many of those employed as paralegals was received on the job. Paralegals entering the field today frequently are taught both legal procedure and substantive law at paralegal programs in educational institutions. These programs are offered by colleges and a variety of proprietary institutions.

The role of paralegals in delivering legal services has been steadily increasing since the late 1970s. According to the 2014–2015 *Occupational Outlook Handbook*, the U.S. Department of Labor estimates that approximately 277,000 individuals held positions as paralegals or legal assistants in 2012. The *Handbook* predicts that employment of paralegals and legal assistants will grow "17 percent between 2012 and 2022, much faster than the average for all occupations."[8]

▶ THE ABA AND PARALEGALS

The ABA has been actively involved in supporting the paralegal profession by encouraging paralegal education and employment. Paralegals are eligible to become associate members of the ABA and are encouraged to become associates in one or more of the 30 ABA Sections and Forums. Associate status in any of these entities entitles one to all privileges of membership except the right to vote or to be an officer or council member. Associate members receive publications and participate in a variety of programs. They are also eligible to be appointed to committees of these entities.

In 1968, the ABA House of Delegates adopted a resolution creating a committee, now named the Standing Committee on Paralegals, to consider professional development and increased education and employment of paralegals to enable lawyers to deliver legal services to the public more effectively. Under the auspices of the ABA House of Delegates, the committee conducts a voluntary program through which paralegal education programs may obtain ABA approval. Currently, there are approximately 250 such approved education programs.

Although the committee is a proponent of formal paralegal education, it also recognizes the value of experience. Guideline G-102 of the *Guidelines for the Approval of Paralegal Education Programs* implicitly acknowledges that other training methods exist: "there should be a number of ways in which a person can demonstrate competence as a paralegal, *one of which is the completion of an approved program.* . . ."[9]

Joining Professional Organizations

▼ To further their own professionalism, paralegals can become involved in the following organizations:

▶ National Association of Legal Assistants (NALA), (918) 587-6828, http://nala.org

▶ National Federation of Paralegal Associations (NFPA), (425) 967-0045, http://www.paralegals.org

▶ American Bar Association (ABA) as an associate member, (800) 285-2221, http://www.americanbar.org/aba.html

---

♦ Paralegal Associations

There are several organizations that represent paralegals and are concerned specifically with development of the paralegal profession. Membership in NALA and NFPA constitutes approximately one-third of the nation's practicing paralegals. Approximately 95 percent of the paralegals represented by these associations work in private law firms or corporations.

In addition, there are two allied professional associations—the American Association for Paralegal Education (AAfPE) and the International Practice Management Association (IPMA). AAfPE's membership includes hundreds of universities, colleges, private schools, and institutions of higher learning throughout the country.[10] IPMA represents paralegal managers who have assumed supervisory responsibilities over other paralegals in traditional law firm settings.

◆ PROFESSIONALISM AND THE PARALEGAL

As members of a legal services delivery team, both lawyer and paralegal should conduct themselves according to the applicable rules of professional conduct and treat one another with respect as colleagues and professionals. This means reaching beyond the rules to develop a personal commitment to professionalism in the workplace.

How is professionalism defined? In 1986, the ABA Commission on Professionalism (informally called the Stanley Commission) wrestled with that question before issuing the report *In the Spirit of Public Service: A Blueprint for the Rekindling of Lawyer Professionalism*.[11] Although the Stanley Commission said that the concept of professionalism was elastic, it decided that the term was so important that a working definition of professionalism was essential.[12] The commission believed the spirit of professionalism was captured by Harvard Law School dean Roscoe Pound in 1953 when he said of a profession:

> The term refers to a group . . . pursuing a learned art as a common calling in the spirit of public service—no less a public service because it may incidentally be a means of livelihood. Pursuit of the learned art in the spirit of a public service is the primary purpose.[13]

The concept of the practice of law "in the spirit of public service" is essential not just for lawyers but for all participants in the delivery of legal services. The ideal of participation by paralegals in the professionalism of the legal community requires more than specialized skills and particular expertise.

Practicing professionalism means caring about how clients are served. It means taking personal responsibility and maintaining high standards in the quality of work. Professionalism includes a mature attitude that results in treating clients, opponents, coworkers, and oneself with dignity and respect. By practicing professionalism, paralegals enhance both the paralegal profession and the legal community.

CHAPTER SUMMARY

- ☑ A paralegal may perform duties such as conducting factual investigation, including locating and interviewing witnesses; assisting with depositions, interrogatories, and document production; compiling statistical and financial data; checking legal citations; and drafting correspondence.

- ☑ Because tasks performed by paralegals are billed at a lower rate than they would be if performed by lawyers, using paralegal services can save the client money and increase access to legal services for low- and middle-income clients.

- ☑ The paralegal should perform tasks competently, refrain from giving legal advice or otherwise engaging in the unauthorized practice of law, and keep the lawyer informed of progress on assignments.

- ☑ Both the lawyer and the paralegal should conduct themselves with professionalism and according to applicable rules of professional conduct.

- ☑ Professionalism includes a mature attitude that results in treating clients, opponents, coworkers, and oneself with dignity and respect.

♦ NOTES

1. LEVERAGING WITH LEGAL ASSISTANTS: HOW TO MAXIMIZE TEAM PERFORMANCE, IMPROVE QUALITY, AND BOOST YOUR BOTTOM LINE (Arthur G. Greene ed., ABA Section of Law Practice Mgmt. 1993).

2. *See* Fla. Registered Paralegal Program r. 20-7.1(c) ("A Florida Registered Paralegal should understand the attorney's Rules of Professional Conduct and this code in order to avoid any action that would involve the attorney in a violation of the rules or give the appearance of professional impropriety. It is the obligation of the Florida Registered Paralegal to avoid conduct that would cause the lawyer to be unethical or even appear to be unethical, and loyalty to the lawyer is incumbent upon the Florida Registered Paralegal.").

3. *See, e.g.*, Fla. Registered Paralegal Program, Ohio Paralegal Certification Program.

4. Adopted by the ABA House of Delegates, August 1997.

5. *See* Missouri v. Jenkins, 491 U.S. 274 (1989).

6. *Id.* at 288 n.10.

7. Susan Mae McCabe, *A Brief History of the Paralegal Profession*, MICH. B.J., July 2007, at 19, *available at* www.michbar.org/journal/pdf/pdf4article1177.pdf.

8. BUREAU OF LABOR STATISTICS, OCCUPATIONAL OUTLOOK HANDBOOK (2014–15 ed.), *available at* http://www.bls.gov/ooh/legal/paralegals-and-legal-assistants.htm.

9. GUIDELINES FOR THE APPROVAL OF PARALEGAL EDUCATION PROGRAMS 3 (effective as amended Sept. 1, 2008) (emphasis added).

10. *See* AM. ASS'N PARALEGAL EDUC., http://www.aafpe.org/AAfPE/American_Association_for_Paralegal_Education.asp.

11. This report was published in 112 F.R.D. 243 (1986). The report was not submitted to the ABA House of Delegates for consideration and is therefore not to be viewed as ABA policy, except as otherwise enacted by the House of Delegates.

12. *Id.* at 261.

13. ROSCOE POUND, THE LAWYER FROM ANTIQUITY TO MODERN TIMES 5 (1953).

Chapter TWO

The Legal Services Delivery Team

- Paralegals and other support staff can contribute significantly to law firm profitability and productivity. Supervising the work of paralegals or other staff, however, involves more than the mere oversight of their work product by the lawyers.

To utilize staff services effectively, it is crucial to include staff members in the communication chain so that they understand firm policies and procedures regarding the ethical rules by which their employers are bound. Failure to do so can bring serious consequences.

As discussed in Chapter 1, the relationship between lawyer and paralegal needs to be based upon cooperation and mutual respect. Except for the prohibition of unauthorized practice of law found in a jurisdiction's statutes, the conduct of paralegals is not regulated. Because of this, the responsibility for ensuring the paralegal's ethical conduct lies with the employing and supervising lawyer.

SUPERVISION OF THE PARALEGAL

ABA Model Rule 5.3 requires a lawyer with direct supervisory authority over a nonlawyer to make reasonable efforts to ensure that the assistant's conduct is compatible with the lawyer's professional obligations.[1] Failure to do so can result in disciplinary proceedings against the lawyer.

Adequate supervision often entails answering the paralegal's questions, overseeing the paralegal's work to confirm that he or she comprehends the assignment, and reviewing the paralegal's work to ensure that it is accurate. The lawyer's supervision should be sufficiently hands-on so that a merger of the paralegal's and lawyer's work product occurs.[2]

In order to help the lawyer fulfill this supervisory responsibility, it is important that the paralegal cooperate with the lawyer and act in a way that is consistent with the lawyer's duties. Thus, the paralegal should ask for clarification and direction whenever a question arises. The paralegal also should be sure to complete any work product long enough before its deadline to allow the lawyer time to carefully review the work.

A lawyer using a paralegal's services is responsible for determining that the paralegal is qualified to perform the tasks assigned, and the paralegal has a duty to support this responsibility as well. Courts have held that lawyers need to make an effort to evaluate a staff member's qualifications to perform the desired work.[3] The paralegal should be honest and forthright about his or her background, qualifications, and level of knowledge to perform assigned tasks. Failure to do so may result in problems for the lawyer and the paralegal.

Careful selection, hiring, and training of paralegals are paramount in ensuring that the paralegal has the education and experience required.[4] The lawyer should verify that the paralegal has the legal research, critical thinking, drafting, organization, and communication skills required to perform substantive work.

The legal basis of the lawyer's obligation to the client for the conduct of a paralegal is the law of agency. Courts have consistently found that secretaries and a variety of other persons act as agents for lawyers employing them and that lawyers are therefore responsible for their staff members' work product.[5]

The 1969 ABA Model Code of Professional Responsibility, predecessor to the Model Rules of Professional Conduct, acknowledged that a lawyer may delegate appropriate tasks to clerks, secretaries, and other laypersons, finding that "[s]uch delegation is proper if the lawyer maintains a direct relationship with [the] client, supervises the delegated work, and has complete professional responsibility for the work product."[6] The Model Code went on to encourage such delegation as a way to enable lawyers to render legal services more economically and efficiently.

Rule 5.3 of the ABA Model Rules of Professional Conduct imposes a more detailed responsibility upon lawyers in their use of nonlawyers (which would include paralegals).[7] The rule requires not only that a supervising lawyer make reasonable efforts to ensure that the nonlawyer's conduct complies with the lawyer's ethical obligations but also that the firm partners, who may or may not have direct supervisory authority, make such efforts to ensure that the firm as a whole has procedures that reasonably ensure the same ethical conduct by its lawyers and nonlawyers.[8]

The commentary to Model Rule 5.3 provides examples of how lawyers may do this, suggesting, for example, that lawyers specifically instruct their nonlawyer assistants about the ethical considerations that are a part of their employment. Lawyers can follow this suggestion by instituting an in-house training program to inform nonlawyer assistants of ethical obligations and rules of legal ethics applicable in the jurisdiction. (See the sidebar "Creating an Ethical Culture," page 14.)

Lawyers also may find guidance in their efforts to ensure ethical behavior by paralegals in the ABA *Model Guidelines for the Utilization of Paralegal Services*. (See the list of guidelines in the sidebar "The ABA's Guidelines on Using Paralegal Services," pages 16–17.) Similar guidelines have been adopted by individual states.[9]

It is important for a paralegal to be familiar with the lawyer's ethical responsibilities because the lawyer is subject to discipline for conduct of the paralegal that the lawyer ordered or permitted and that the lawyer is ethically prohibited from performing on his or her own.[10]

> **Creating an Ethical Culture**
>
> ▼ An effective, ongoing, in-house program of ethics may include the following:
>
> ► an orientation program to explain basic legal ethics
>
> ► periodic seminars that illustrate how ethics principles operate in the context of real-life decision-making situations
>
> ► an open-door policy, fostering open communications between paralegals and lawyer supervisors, to allow an exchange of ideas and concerns throughout the firm
>
> ► periodic ethics surveys to monitor compliance
>
> These tools should be used to create and maintain a law firm culture in which the observance of appropriate ethical values and conduct is institutionalized.

♦ OFFICE PROCEDURES

Office procedures are often delegated to paralegals, office managers, and other nonlawyer staff. This delegation is proper as long as lawyers provide adequate supervision and remain accountable for the procedures. In fact, courts have acknowledged that a lawyer's delegation of work is essential to the efficient operation of any law office.[11]

On the other hand, as a review of lawyer discipline cases readily reveals, lawyers may be disciplined for negligent office management practices, including failure to oversee and supervise routine acts such as handling phone messages and mail. Delegation by the lawyer is not the same as relinquishing responsibility for the office. Supervision is still critical to protect the interests of clients. The lawyer must set up safeguards to ensure proper administration of the matters entrusted to the lawyer by his or her clients.

In one case, for example, a lawyer was disciplined for failure to communicate with clients, sign forms, forward client files promptly, and promptly endorse and return a former client's settlement draft. The lawyer's office manager had hidden information so that a mere review of office files may not have revealed the needed information. At the disciplinary hearing, the lawyer acknowledged that he was responsible for the reasonable supervision of his staff.[12]

Thus, it is important that a paralegal who cannot keep up with the workload let the supervising lawyer know and not try to hide the problem. In addition, if the paralegal sees that the lawyer is letting things fall behind to the point of creating problems, the paralegal should not hide the situation in an attempt to relieve the lawyer's burden.

In another case, a lawyer was disbarred for abandoning responsibility for running his law practice. The lawyer did not screen, instruct, or supervise his employees. To further confuse matters, he signed pages of blank checks, thus allowing the employees to decide whether and how much to pay clients from their trust accounts.[13] A paralegal should not look upon a lawyer's derogation of duty as a sign of confidence in the paralegal and should not assume responsibilities that are not delegable. Instead, the paralegal should remind the lawyer when assigned actions are not delegable.

Another lawyer was suspended for, among other things, failing to properly supervise his paralegal, who placed a newspaper advertisement for the law firm that contained language that violated the state's rules of professional conduct. As stated by the court, "[l]awyers should give legal assistants appropriate instruction and supervision concerning legal aspects of their employment, taking into account the fact that they do not have legal training."[14]

In another case, a lawyer turned control of his client trust account over to his wife, who was his secretary and bookkeeper. The wife would "borrow" funds from the trust account to pay the office bills. The lawyer was disciplined for improper delegation of signatory power and failure to supervise the account.[15] This case illustrates that the fact that the nonlawyer assistant may be related to the supervising lawyer does not change either's ethical responsibilities.

The ABA's Guidelines on Using Paralegal Services

▼ The ABA's *Model Guidelines for the Utilization of Paralegal Services* states:

► Guideline 1: A lawyer is responsible for all of the professional actions of a paralegal performing services at the lawyer's direction and should take reasonable measures to ensure that the paralegal's conduct is consistent with the lawyer's obligations under the rules of professional conduct of the jurisdiction in which the lawyer practices.

► Guideline 2: Provided the lawyer maintains responsibility for the work product, a lawyer may delegate to a paralegal any task normally performed by the lawyer except those tasks proscribed to a nonlawyer by statute, court rule, administrative rule or regulation, controlling authority, the applicable rule of professional conduct of the jurisdiction in which the lawyer practices, or these Guidelines.

► Guideline 3: A lawyer may not delegate to a paralegal:
  (a) Responsibility for establishing an attorney-client relationship.
  (b) Responsibility for establishing the amount of a fee to be charged for a legal service.
  (c) Responsibility for a legal opinion rendered to a client.

► Guideline 4: A lawyer is responsible for taking reasonable measures to ensure that clients, courts, and other lawyers are aware that a paralegal, whose services are utilized by the lawyer in performing legal services, is not licensed to practice law.

Another lawyer completely delegated banking and bookkeeping control to his office manager without instructing him on trust account requirements and procedures. In addition, the lawyer never reviewed the records or the bank statements for any of the office accounts. The Court found a pattern of gross negligence involving serious violations of the lawyer's duty to

Continued from previous page

▶ Guideline 5: A lawyer may identify paralegals by name and title on the lawyer's letterhead and on business cards identifying the lawyer's firm.

▶ Guideline 6: A lawyer is responsible for taking reasonable measures to ensure that all client confidences are preserved by a paralegal.

▶ Guideline 7: A lawyer should take reasonable measures to prevent conflicts of interest resulting from a paralegal's other employment or interests.

▶ Guideline 8: A lawyer may include a charge for the work performed by a paralegal in setting a charge and/or billing for legal services.

▶ Guideline 9: A lawyer may not split legal fees with a paralegal nor pay a paralegal for the referral of legal business. A lawyer may compensate a paralegal based on the quantity and quality of the paralegal's work and the value of that work to a law practice, but the paralegal's compensation may not be contingent, by advance agreement, upon the outcome of a particular case or class of cases.

▶ Guideline 10: A lawyer who employs a paralegal should facilitate the paralegal's participation in appropriate continuing education and pro bono publico activities.

oversee client funds entrusted to his care.[16] Proper supervision includes adequate instruction when assigning, monitoring, and reviewing projects. The lawyer must not assume the paralegal will know how to handle a task properly simply because the paralegal has experience working for another lawyer. When accepting procedural assignments, the paralegal should inform the supervising lawyer if the paralegal is not properly prepared to execute the tasks.

◆ SUBSTANTIVE ASSIGNMENTS

As noted previously, Guideline 2 of the *Model Guidelines* approves a lawyer's delegating to a paralegal any task normally performed by the lawyer "except those tasks proscribed to a nonlawyer by statute, court rule, administrative rule or regulation, controlling authority, the applicable rule of professional conduct of the jurisdiction in which the lawyer practices, or these Guidelines" as long as the lawyer maintains responsibility for the work product. Indeed, the U.S. Supreme Court has recognized that the variety of tasks being performed by paralegals facilitates the cost-effective delivery of legal services.[17] Paralegals who are meaningfully integrated into the lawyer's practice will be offered a variety of substantive assignments.

Paralegal involvement in substantive legal work, through researching case precedent, writing up results, and even expressing an opinion as to the strengths of a case to the supervising lawyer (but never to the client), is not to be confused with "practicing law." Indeed, Model Rule 5.5 and most jurisdictions' rules specifically prohibit lawyers from assisting or aiding a nonlawyer in the unauthorized practice of law. A lawyer's failure to properly supervise a paralegal can result in discipline against the lawyer if the conduct results in the paralegal engaging in the unauthorized practice of law.[18]

Thus, when a paralegal is working on client matters, the lawyer must ensure that the paralegal does not give independent advice on substantive legal issues. Even advice that may seem innocuous, such as instructions from the paralegal to the client on procedural matters or advice on how to fill out forms, has been found by the courts to constitute the unauthorized practice of law.[19] With this caution in mind, it is nevertheless true that paralegals often play an important role in improving communications between the lawyer and the client, and should be allowed to serve as a conduit of information between them.

How far a lawyer should go in delegating work to a paralegal, even within the bounds of generally acceptable guidelines, must be related to the amount of supervision the lawyer will be able to exercise and the experience and training of the paralegal. It is both acceptable and desirable for a lawyer who has worked extensively with a paralegal to exercise a lesser degree of supervision over the paralegal. However, the paralegal must be prepared to identify unfamiliar situations and ask for instructions from the supervising lawyer when such situations arise.

Lawyers may sometimes forget the limitations on paralegals, asking them to perform tasks that are not permitted. The qualified paralegal should therefore develop an independent understanding of what he or she may legally and ethically do and be prepared to remind the lawyer of the limitations of the paralegal's position.[20]

▶ SPECIFIC PROHIBITIONS AND CONCERNS

Deciding what work can be delegated to a paralegal is not always an easy task. State courts, bar associations, and bar committees in several states have prepared recommendations for the utilization of paralegals to provide a reliable basis for delegating responsibility for some legal tasks. Because recommendations vary from jurisdiction to jurisdiction, it is necessary for paralegals to become familiar with guidelines in use where they are employed.

Although the responsibilities given to paralegals have increased over time and paralegals are now routinely engaged in some activities that until recently were perceived to be the exclusive province of lawyers, there remain some actions that a paralegal is not permitted to undertake as being the unauthorized practice of law. Among these are the following:

- establishing a client-lawyer relationship
- establishing the amount of a fee to be charged for a legal service
- rendering a legal opinion to a client
- representing a party in court

These tasks all require the exercise of a lawyer's professional judgment.

Other actions that a paralegal should be careful not to engage in include the following:

- preparing or filing documents on behalf of the supervising lawyer without the lawyer's knowledge, approval, or review

- communicating with a client without the lawyer's knowledge
- withholding information from the lawyer regarding the status of matters (covering up neglect can only lead to further, more serious problems)

Finally, while closely supervising every act of a paralegal is impractical for a lawyer and would defeat the purpose of employing an assistant, the paralegal should have legitimate concerns regarding a breach of supervision when the paralegal is any of the following:

- authorized to sign office checking accounts, client trust accounts, or lawyer/fiduciary accounts
- given sole responsibility for balancing bank statements without supervisory review
- permitted by the firm to sign a lawyer's name on letters and pleadings
- permitted to file papers without a lawyer's review

♦ Conclusion

Newly hired paralegals should be provided with a copy and an explanation of the ethical rules of the jurisdiction in which they will be practicing. The lawyer has a formal responsibility to ensure that the paralegal does not engage in the unauthorized practice of law and may be disciplined for failing to fulfill it. The paralegal has an obligation to be aware of what is ethically permissible and to call to the lawyer's attention any situations that may arise in which the paralegal is being asked to engage in impermissible activities.

CHAPTER SUMMARY

☑ A lawyer using a paralegal's services is responsible for determining that the paralegal is qualified to perform the tasks assigned.

- ☑ Some courts and bar associations have developed guidelines for delegating responsibility to paralegals.

- ☑ Model Rule 5.3 requires that a supervising lawyer make reasonable efforts to ensure that a nonlawyer's conduct complies with the lawyer's ethical obligations.

- ☑ A lawyer may not delegate to a paralegal (1) responsibility for establishing a client-lawyer relationship, (2) responsibility for establishing the amount of a fee to be charged for a legal service, or (3) responsibility for a legal opinion rendered to a client.

- ☑ Lawyers may be disciplined for negligent office management practices.

- ☑ A paralegal must be prepared to identify unfamiliar situations and ask for instructions from the supervising lawyer when such situations arise.

- ☑ A paralegal should not attempt to hide problems for any reason.

- ☑ A paralegal should not accept nondelegable duties.

- ☑ A paralegal should develop an independent understanding of what he or she may legally and ethically do and be prepared to remind the lawyer of the limitations of the paralegal's position.

♦ Notes

1. Model Rules of Prof'l Conduct R. 5.3(b) (2013); see In re Schelly, 446 N.E.2d 236 (Ill. 1983).

2. See In re Jorissen, 391 N.W.2d 822 (Minn. 1986).

3. For example, in the case of In re Scanlan, 697 P.2d 1084 (Ariz. 1985), a lawyer was suspended for 90 days for negligently allowing a secretary to embezzle funds from client trust accounts. If the lawyer had checked the employment history of the secretary, he would have learned that the secretary had stolen money from two previous employers and was under indictment for forgery and theft of funds.

4. See Diane Petropulos, Hiring the Perfect Paralegal, Cal. Paralegal, Apr.–June 1992, at 27.

5. See, e.g., State v. Barrett, 483 P.2d 1106 (Kan. 1971) (court disbarred a lawyer for commingling funds and failing to fulfill trust obligations despite the lawyer's suggestion that some of the problems may have resulted from actions taken by his employees).

6. Model Code of Prof'l Responsibility EC 3-6 (1980).

7. The ABA Model Rules of Professional Conduct replaced the ABA Model Code of Professional Responsibility in 1983 and are now in effect (as variously amended) in every jurisdiction except California.

8. ABA Model Rule 5.3 reads in full:

Responsibility Regarding Nonlawyer Assistance

With respect to a nonlawyer employed or retained by or associated with a lawyer:

(a) a partner, and a lawyer who individually or together with other lawyers possesses comparable managerial authority in a law firm shall make reasonable efforts to ensure that the firm has in effect measures giving reasonable assurance that the person's conduct is compatible with the professional obligations of the lawyer;

(b) a lawyer having direct supervisory authority over the nonlawyer shall make reasonable effort to ensure that the person's conduct is compatible with the professional obligation of the lawyer; and

(c) a lawyer shall be responsible for conduct of such a person that would be a violation of the Rules of Professional Conduct if engaged by a lawyer if:

   (1) the lawyer orders or, with the knowledge of the specific conduct, ratifies the conduct involved; or

   (2) the lawyer is a partner or has comparable managerial authority in the law firm in which the person is employed, or has direct supervisory authority over the person, and knows of the conduct at a time when its consequences can be avoided or mitigated but fails to take reasonable remedial action.

9. *See, e.g.*, Idaho State Bar Model Guidelines for the Utilization of Legal Assistant Services (1992), *available at* http://isb.idaho.gov/pdf/general/legasst.pdf; Ind. Rules of Prof'l Conduct: Use of Non-lawyer Assistants, *available at* http://www.in.gov/judiciary/rules/prof_conduct/#_USE_OF_NON-LAWYER_ASSISTANTS; Kan. Bar, Official Standards and Guidelines for the Utilization of Legal Assistants/Paralegals in Kansas (as amended Feb. 2004), *available at* http://www.nala.org/KSG_04.pdf; State Bar of Mich., Role of Nonlawyers in Law Practice: Guidelines for the Utilization of Legal Assistant Services (rev. 1993), *available at* http://www.michbar.org/opinions/ethics/utilization.cfm; Mo. Bar, Practicing with Paralegals (2003), *available at* http://www.mobar.org/uploadedFiles/Home/Publications/Legal_Resources/Brochures_and_Booklets/paralegals.pdf; N.H. Sup. Ct. R. 35 (1987), *available at* http://www.courts.state.nh.us/rules/scr/scr-35.htm; N.M. Sup. Ct. Order No. 04-8300 (2004), *available at* http://www.nmbar.org/NmbarDocs/AboutUs/ParalegalDivision/RulesGoverningParalegalServices.pdf (Rules Governing Paralegal Services); S.D. Codified Laws § 16-18-34.2 (Utilization of Legal Assistants), *available at* http://legis.sd.gov/Statutes/Codified_Laws/DisplayStatute.aspx?Type=Statute&Statute=16-18-34.2; Utah State Bar, Guidelines for the Utilization of Paralegals, Rules of Integration and Management R. C24, *available at* http://paralegals.utahbar.org/index.php/Utilization_Guidelines.

10. *See* MODEL RULES OF PROF'L CONDUCT R. 5.3(c) (2013).
11. Office of Disciplinary Counsel v. Ball, 618 N.E.2d 159 (Ohio 1993).
12. *In re* Kaplan, 1993 WL 330653 (Cal. Bar Ct. 1993).
13. *In re* Struthers, 877 P.2d 789 (Ariz. 1994).
14. *In re* Cartmel, 676 N.E.2d 1047, 1051 (Ind. 1997).
15. *In re* Stransky, 612 A.2d 373 (N.J. 1992); *see also In re* Anonymous, 876 N.E.2d 333 (Ind. 2007).
16. Palomo v. State Bar, 685 P.2d 1185 (Cal. 1984); *see also In re* Bailey, 821 A.2d 851 (Del. 2003).
17. *See* Missouri v. Jenkins, 491 U.S. 274, n.10 (1989).
18. *See* State v. Fry, 875 P.2d 222 (Colo. 1994).
19. *See* State v. Consumer Sounding Bd., 834 P.2d 467 (Or. 1992).
20. LEVERAGING WITH LEGAL ASSISTANTS: HOW TO MAXIMIZE TEAM PERFORMANCE, IMPROVE QUALITY, AND BOOST YOUR BOTTOM LINE (Arthur G. Greene ed., ABA Section of Law Practice Mgmt. 1993).

Chapter THREE

The Law of Professional Responsibility

♦ RULES FOR PARALEGALS

Rules of professional conduct clarify and mandate what is expected of legal professionals in various situations. They are written to protect the public and to help inspire public trust in the legal profession. State regulations protect consumers by requiring of lawyers a threshold level of skill and professional judgment and placing ethical constraints on lawyers in their delivery of services. By and large, no parallel state regulations apply to nonlawyers working in the legal services field. A few states—Arizona, California, New Mexico, and Washington—have forms of regulation related to paralegals and other nonlawyers involved in providing legal services.[1] Some other states have adopted a variety of voluntary rules.[2]

Even though enforceable codified ethics rules for paralegals do not exist at this time, the National Association of Legal Assistants and the National Federation of Paralegal Associations have recognized the importance of creating guidelines and standards of professional conduct specifically for paralegals. As a result, both NALA and NFPA have adopted model codes of ethics to help guide paralegal conduct in the delivery of legal services.[3] In addition, some states have promulgated their own rules directed toward paralegals, though these are not enforceable.[4]

There are also rules of professional conduct for lawyers, adopted by the highest court in every jurisdiction, that are of great importance to paralegals. Paralegals must know and follow these rules in order to behave ethically in the legal world. Canon 10 of the NALA Code of Ethics and Professional Responsibility states that a paralegal's conduct is guided by lawyer codes of professional responsibility and rules of professional conduct.

Also, as agents of lawyers, paralegals are expected to act in compliance with the lawyers' rules of professional conduct because, in many instances, their conduct can be attributed to their employing lawyers.[5] And a paralegal's unethical conduct can have severe consequences not only for the paralegal and the lawyer but also for clients and other members of the public, as will be discussed.

The balance of this handbook explains these professional conduct rules and offers guidance on how paralegals can conform their conduct to these rules.

▶ Evolution of Rules of Professional Conduct

A brief history of rules of professional conduct may be helpful to understand their status today. In 1887, Alabama became the first jurisdiction to adopt a code of ethics for lawyers. In 1908, the ABA used this code as the basis of its Canons of Professional Ethics, which consisted of general statements of expected conduct. The ABA Canons were adopted by many jurisdictions and were later integrated into various statutes and court rules.

The ABA revised the Canons in 1969. The result was the ABA Model Code of Professional Responsibility, which contained general concepts (Canons), rules (Disciplinary Rules), and aspirational comments (Ethical Considerations). This ethics code was replaced in 1983, when the ABA adopted the current Model Rules of Professional Conduct. The Model Rules consist of enforceable black-letter rules and are supplemented with interpretive comments. The Model Rules continue to be amended as changes occur in the everyday practice of law or, as on occasion happens, courts find them otherwise in need of revision.

♦ Local Rules

As the name implies, the Model Rules serve as a model for the professional conduct standards adopted in the individual jurisdictions. Each jurisdiction adopts its own set of rules, which become the law governing lawyer conduct in that jurisdiction. This means that lawyers in that jurisdiction will be bound by those rules and can be disciplined for failure to comply with them. Although the ABA Model Rules have been adopted in some form by every jurisdiction except California, most of those adopting the rules have not done so word for word; frequently, additions or deletions have been made to reflect local dispositions on the more controversial provisions. Thus, it is very important for a paralegal to know his or her jurisdiction's rules.

In most states, the highest court of the jurisdiction (usually called the supreme court) is responsible for adopting rules relating generally to the practice of law. Thus, these courts adopt not only rules of professional conduct but also requirements for admission to the practice of law and procedural rules for lawyer discipline.

In addition to supreme court rules, most jurisdictions have legislative statutes that govern who can practice law. These statutes typically provide criminal and civil penalties for certain types of conduct, including the unauthorized practice of law by those who are not lawyers. Moreover, lawyers are prohibited from assisting nonlawyers in the unauthorized practice of law. Therefore, the paralegal must take care to ensure that all legal work he or she performs is properly supervised by a lawyer. The unauthorized practice of law may include actions such as representing clients, setting legal fees, drafting legal documents, or giving legal advice without a law license. The range of prohibited conduct varies from one jurisdiction to another.

The highest court of each jurisdiction is also the body that enforces the rules of professional conduct. However, although the Model Rules are not designed to be a basis for civil liability, the lower courts also may refer to and apply the rules when deciding civil and criminal cases. For example, lower courts can rule on the reasonableness and collectability of fees, applying both the language and spirit of the Model Rule governing that subject. They also may refer to the Model Rules regarding conflicts of interest in deciding whether to disqualify a lawyer from handling a case or to the Model Rule on competence in deciding whether to hold a lawyer liable for malpractice. In addition, most courts establish local rules of practice that lawyers must become familiar with when appearing before the court.

Ethics opinions are an additional form of guidance for the practice of law. They interpret the directives found in rules of professional conduct. Issued by the ABA and by state and local bar associations, ethics opinions do not have the authority that supreme court rules and statutes have, but they are an important resource for those who work in the legal profession. Copies of state or local ethics opinions usually can be obtained from a jurisdiction's lawyer regulatory agency or from the committee of the bar specially appointed to provide information about legal ethics issues. The ABA maintains a web page that links to many of the opinions.[6]

◆ THE RULE BREAKERS

Lawyers who violate ethics rules are disciplined by sanctions. The sanction to be imposed, if any, is initially determined by a disciplinary agency established by a jurisdiction's highest court. After an initial recommendation for discipline by the agency, the matter is referred to the jurisdiction's highest court, which imposes the recommended sanction, imposes a lesser or greater sanction, or dismisses the matter.

Sanctions include private and public reprimand, admonition, suspension from the practice of law for a set period (with or without probation), and disbarment. The mildest sanction, a private reprimand, is communicated only to the lawyer being reprimanded. Disbarment, the strictest sanction, is the revocation of the license to practice law. Some jurisdictions permit a disbarred lawyer to petition to be readmitted to practice after a specific number of years (often five).

The Law of Professional Responsibility

For paralegals, there presently is no corresponding mechanism for professional discipline. Paralegals presently have no state regulations and no set criteria to define the requirements of and barriers to practice as a paralegal. Nor is there any form of public regulation designed to ensure that paralegals perform their duties in a competent manner. Paralegals do not have licenses that can be suspended or revoked. Their ethics concepts are aspirational only, presented in the form of statements of principle. Examples of these are the codes of ethics developed by both NFPA and NALA.[7]

Many jurisdictions have adopted guidelines for lawyers to follow in using the services of paralegals, although these are not binding.[8] These guidelines frequently cover the interactions of paralegals with lawyers, clients, and the public. They also address such subjects as the unauthorized practice of law, disclosure of paralegal status, confidentiality, conflicts of interest, supervision, delegation of responsibility, and financial arrangements between lawyers and paralegals.

In August 1991, the ABA adopted its own *Model Guidelines for the Utilization of Legal Assistant Services* to encourage the appropriate use of paralegals in the practice of law. (In 2004, these guidelines were amended and renamed the ABA *Model Guidelines for the Utilization of Paralegal Services* "to conform with the most common term used in the legal community and educational institutions." See Appendix C for a complete copy of the *Model Guidelines*.) Under the *Model Guidelines*, a lawyer may delegate to a paralegal only work supervised by a lawyer that does not require the paralegal to render legal advice or exercise a lawyer's professional judgment.

▶ CONSEQUENCES OF MISCONDUCT

Although a paralegal cannot be officially reprimanded, suspended, or disbarred, there nonetheless are harmful consequences for failure to comply with ethical requirements. One likely consequence of unethical conduct by a paralegal may be the loss of employment. Lawyers are required by their own rules to demand strict observance of ethical requirements by paralegals they employ, and therefore lawyers are likely to consider an ethics breach more than sufficient grounds to terminate employment.

A paralegal's unethical conduct may expose the lawyer/employer to serious harm. Lawyers today practice in a very competitive and demanding marketplace. That environment demands that professional legal services be performed efficiently and at a competitive cost.[9] At the very least, unethical conduct or incompetent work by the paralegal will lessen the efficiency of the legal practice of the employing lawyer. Clients who find that their lawyer is not delivering legal services efficiently may go to another lawyer for their legal needs, which again may affect the paralegal's continued employment.

A breach of ethics also may require payment of monetary damages in a civil lawsuit for negligence against the lawyer or paralegal or malpractice against the lawyer. The paralegal's failure to conform to ethical standards may result in specific, demonstrable harm to the client when, for example, the ethical breach consists of disclosure of confidential information, taking a position in conflict with that of the client, practicing law without a license, or performing professional work in a negligent manner.[10] If the client has suffered identifiable personal or economic harm as a consequence of the paralegal's breach of ethics or negligence, the lawyer will, in all probability, be the subject of a damage and/or malpractice action by the disgruntled client.[11] The lawyer is both legally and professionally responsible for the work product and professional conduct of the paralegal.[12]

Further, the employing lawyer may face professional discipline because of the unethical conduct of the paralegal. Unethical conduct by a paralegal is likely to raise a question as to the lawyer's proper supervision of the paralegal. Thus, all instances of the paralegal's failure to meet ethical requirements have the potential to result in disciplinary charges being lodged against the lawyer; indeed, lawyers have been disbarred for failure to supervise paralegals or other nonlawyer staff members who were found to have committed serious ethical misconduct.[13]

Finally, unethical conduct by a lawyer or paralegal may have a negative impact on the public's perception of the legal system, thereby creating issues of trust that affect the legal profession's special responsibilities related to the quality of justice for all.

◆ Reporting Professional Misconduct

What are the responsibilities of paralegals when they find out someone in their law firm has committed an ethical breach? Whether or not to report misconduct, and identifying the appropriate person or entity to notify, may well be among the most difficult decisions a paralegal will be called upon to make. The ramifications of ignoring unethical conduct make it necessary for the paralegal to take action. Questioning the judgment of senior lawyers, however, may seem disloyal to the firm or to an individual lawyer. But while lawyers, paralegals, and other law firm employees owe loyalty to their employers, they also have a duty to obey the law and to help maintain the integrity of the legal profession. Thus, when professional misconduct occurs within a law firm, there is a duty to report the misconduct, as difficult as that may be.[14] The appropriate action to take will depend on a number of factors, including the nature of the conduct, the internal procedures available in the office, and the avenues for reporting misconduct available in the paralegal's jurisdiction.

Taking Action

▼ The options available to a paralegal for reporting unethical conduct include the following:

▶ reporting unethical conduct to a supervising lawyer

▶ reporting unethical conduct to a committee within the law firm, company, or corporation

▶ reporting unethical conduct to the state's lawyer disciplinary agency

▶ reporting an emotional or chemical-dependency problem to a lawyer assistance program

▶ reporting criminal conduct to the local prosecutor's office

EC-1.3(d) of the NFPA Model Code of Ethics and Professional Responsibility provides that "a paralegal shall advise the proper authority of non-confidential knowledge of any action of another legal professional that clearly demonstrates fraud, deceit, dishonesty, or misrepresentation."

As stated above, reporting misconduct is important, but because an allegation of misconduct is a very serious matter, the paralegal should be careful that he or she has sufficient knowledge of the facts before proceeding. Unfortunately, for reporting purposes, there is no clear definition of knowledge. As recognized in the ABA Model Rules, knowledge "may be inferred from circumstances."[15]

Paralegals should first attempt to discuss perceived instances of unethical conduct with their supervising lawyer. In addition, many law firms or legal departments have an internal committee available to review possible misconduct by employees. These committees may be informal or formal, depending on the organization. If the paralegal works for a solo practitioner or is not satisfied with the response within the firm after reporting on the conduct of a lawyer, he or she can contact the local lawyer disciplinary agency to report an instance of misconduct.[16]

If a paralegal has reason to suspect that the lawyer whose conduct is at issue needs assistance with a substance-abuse problem, the paralegal can contact a lawyer assistance program. The ABA Commission on Lawyer Assistance Programs maintains a directory of state programs on its website.[17] The goal of these programs is to help the lawyer who has the problem. All calls to these programs are confidential. Additional information is provided in Chapter 5.

CHAPTER SUMMARY

- ☑ Each jurisdiction has its own rules and statutes regarding lawyer conduct.
- ☑ Ethics opinions from bar associations also provide guidance.
- ☑ Lawyers who violate ethics rules can be prohibited from practicing.

The Law of Professional Responsibility

☑ Lawyers are responsible for supervising their paralegals.

☑ Many jurisdictions have guidelines for lawyers using the services of paralegals.

☑ Unethical conduct by paralegals can lead to loss of employment and personal liability.

☑ Paralegals have a duty to report misconduct.

☑ Help is available for lawyers and paralegals with alcohol or substance-abuse problems.

♦ NOTES

1. See CAL. BUS. & PROF. CODE §§ 6450–6456, available at http://www.leginfo.ca.gov/cgi-bin/displaycode?section=bpc&group=06001-07000&file=6450-6456. Arizona has a Code of Judicial Administration regarding legal document preparers at http://www.azcourts.gov/Portals/0/admcode/pdfcurrentcode/7-208_Amend_2013.pdf. New Mexico has Rules Governing Paralegal Services at http://www.nmbar.org/NmbarDocs/AboutUs/ParalegalDivision/RulesGoverningParalegalServices.pdf. Washington has a Limited Practice Rule for Limited License Legal Technicians at http://www.wsba.org/Legal-Community/Committees-Boards-and-Other-Groups/Limited-License-Legal-Technician-Board. See also the paralegal licensing program of the Law Society of Upper Canada and the Paralegal Rules of Conduct at http://www.lsuc.on.ca/with.aspx?id=1072. Paralegals in Ontario are permitted to provide some services that require a law license in the United States. In its first year of paralegal regulation, the Law Society issued over 2,000 paralegal licenses. Paralegals who provide legal services to the public must carry professional liability insurance. See http://rc.lsuc.on.ca/jsp/home/paralegalindex.jsp for all the details of the licensing program.

2. See Regulation Chart by State, NAT'L FED'N PARALEGAL ASS'N, http://www.paralegals.org/default.asp?page=30 (last visited Nov. 15, 2013).

3. See NAT'L ASS'N OF LEGAL ASSISTANTS, CODE OF ETHICS AND PROFESSIONAL RESPONSIBILITY (2007), available in Appendix A and at http://www.nala.org/code.aspx; NAT'L FED'N OF PARALEGAL ASS'NS, MODEL DISCIPLINARY RULES AND ETHICAL CONSIDERATIONS (2006), available in Appendix B and at http://www.paralegals.org/associations/2270/files/Model_Code_of_Ethics_09_06.pdt.

4. See, e.g., STATE BAR OF N.M., CODE OF ETHICS AND PROFESSIONAL RESPONSIBILITY, available at http://www.nmbar.org/NmbarDocs/AboutUs/ParalegalDivision/CodeofEthics.pdf; UTAH STATE BAR, CANONS OF ETHICS: PARALEGAL DIVISION,

available at http://paralegals.utahbar.org/data/_uploaded/assets/info/canon_of_ethics.pdf.

5. Ethical conduct is required of paralegals because of their participation in the legal system and is a professional obligation owed to their employer, their employer's clients, and the legal system. See NFPA MODEL CODE OF ETHICS AND PROFESSIONAL RESPONSIBILITY (1993); NALA CODE OF ETHICS AND PROFESSIONAL RESPONSIBILITY (2007).

6. See Links of Interest, ABA, http://www.americanbar.org/groups/professional_responsibility/resources/links_of_interest.html (last visited Apr. 7, 2015).

7. See also LAW SOC'Y OF UPPER CAN., PARALEGAL RULES OF CONDUCT, supra note 1.

8. See, e.g., IDAHO STATE BAR MODEL GUIDELINES FOR THE UTILIZATION OF PARALEGAL SERVICES (1992), available at isb.idaho.gov/pdf/general/legasst.pdf; IND. RULES OF PROF'L CONDUCT: USE OF NON-LAWYER ASSISTANTS, available at http://www.in.gov/judiciary/rules/prof_conduct/#_USE_OF_NON-LAWYER_ASSISTANTS; KAN. BAR, OFFICIAL STANDARDS AND GUIDELINES FOR THE UTILIZATION OF PARALEGALS/PARALEGALS IN KANSAS (as amended Feb. 2004), available at http://www.nala.org/KSG_04.pdf; STATE BAR OF MICH. GUIDELINES FOR THE UTILIZATION OF PARALEGAL SERVICES (rev. 1993), available at http://www.michbar.org/opinions/ethics/utilization.cfm; MO. BAR GUIDELINES FOR PRACTICING WITH PARALEGALS (2003), available at http://www.mobar.org/uploadedFiles/Home/Publications/Legal_Resources/Brochures_and_Booklets/paralegals.pdf; N.H. SUP. CT. R. 35 (1987), available at http://www.courts.state.nh.us/rules/scr/scr-35.htm; N.M. SUP. CT., RULES GOVERNING PARALEGAL SERVICES (2006), available at http://www.nmbar.org/NmbarDocs/AboutUs/ParalegalDivision/RulesGoverningParalegalServices.pdf; S.D. CODIFIED LAWS § 16-18-34.2 (Utilization of Paralegals), available at http://legis.sd.gov/Statutes/Codified_Laws/DisplayStatute.aspx?Type=Statute&Statute=16-18-34.2; UTAH STATE BAR GUIDELINES FOR THE UTILIZATION OF PARALEGALS, available at http://paralegals.utahbar.org/index.php/Utilization_Guidelines.

9. KATHLEEN WILLIAMS-FORTIN, LEVERAGING WITH PARALEGALS (Arthur G. Greene ed., ABA Section of Law Practice Mgmt. 1993).

10. The negligence of a nonlawyer in performing legal tasks can be the basis for personal liability. Biakanja v. Irving, 320 P.2d 16 (Cal. 1958).

11. A malpractice judgment in excess of $240,000 against a lawyer was affirmed. The lawyer failed to properly supervise an employee, and the negligence of the employee resulted in harm to the client. Musselman v. Willoughby Corp., 337 S.E.2d 724 (Va. 1985).

12. ABA MODEL GUIDELINES FOR THE UTILIZATION OF PARALEGAL SERVICES, Guideline 1 (2012).

13. See, e.g., La. State Bar Ass'n v. Edwins, 540 So. 2d 294 (La. 1989); State ex rel Okla. Bar Ass'n v. Taylor, 4 P.3d 1242 (Okla. 2000).

14. See In re Himmel, 533 N.E.2d 790 (Ill. 1988), a case in which a lawyer was disciplined solely for failing to report another lawyer's unethical conduct. Himmel represented a woman in a claim against her prior lawyer for conversion of

settlement funds from a personal injury suit. Himmel negotiated an agreement that provided that the prior lawyer would pay the client $75,000 in settlement of any claims. The agreement provided that no disciplinary action would be initiated against the prior lawyer. The state lawyer disciplinary agency became aware of the settlement, and the prior lawyer was disciplined for conversion. Himmel was publicly reprimanded for failure to report unprivileged information regarding the prior lawyer's misconduct.

15. MODEL RULES OF PROF'L CONDUCT R. 1.0(f) (2013).

16. *See Resources for the Public*, ABA, http://www.americanbar.org/groups/professional_responsibility/resources/resources_for_the_public.html (last visited Apr. 7, 2015).

17. The commission's web page includes a directory of state lawyer assistance programs *at* http://www.americanbar.org/groups/lawyer_assistance/resources/lap_programs_by_state.html.

Chapter FOUR

Unauthorized Practice of Law

♦ THE UNAUTHORIZED PRACTICE OF LAW AND THE PARALEGAL

The ability to practice law legally is not a right but rather a license granted by a government entity. Each jurisdiction sets its own requirements for a license. A license to practice law is, with limited exceptions, restricted to persons who have satisfied certain requirements established by the highest court of a jurisdiction, usually a degree from an accredited law school, a passing score on the jurisdiction's bar examination, and good moral character.

Simply put, paralegals may conduct any law-related services at which they are competent, provided they do not engage in the "unauthorized practice of law." The unauthorized practice of law (UPL) is the practice of law by someone who does not hold a current law license.

Just because a lawyer often performs a certain function does not necessarily make it the practice of law. Both lawyers and paralegals often fill in blanks on standardized forms, handle routine telephone calls from clients, and maintain legal files. But paralegals are rapidly becoming skilled at providing an ever-increasing range of law-related services, and therefore identifying which services require a lawyer's expertise is important.

While the UPL standard is easy to articulate, it is difficult to apply. One reason is that the definition of the practice of law varies from jurisdiction to jurisdiction and can be quite vague. Another reason is that the line between legal services properly conducted by paralegals and the unauthorized practice of law often has been a matter of contention between various groups in the legal community.

UPL Rules

ABA Model Rule of Professional Conduct 5.5 forbids a lawyer from assisting another, including a nonlawyer, in the unauthorized practice of law.[1] It does not define the practice of law, leaving that to the individual jurisdictions.[2] As noted earlier, every jurisdiction has one or more laws prohibiting the unauthorized practice of law; in most places, it is a misdemeanor punishable by fine or imprisonment.

According to Canon 3 of the NALA Code of Ethics and Professional Responsibility, a paralegal shall not engage in the unauthorized practice of law. EC-1.8(a) of the NFPA Model Code of Ethics and Professional Responsibility provides that a paralegal shall comply with the applicable legal authority governing the unauthorized practice of law. All of these rules allow a lawyer to delegate certain work to qualified paralegals as long as the lawyer supervises the work and retains responsibility for the work product.

Because the paralegal's work is dependent upon the lawyer's supervision, the lawyer must be in a position to assume responsibility for the work. Thus, for example, if the lawyer's license has been suspended, the paralegal may not continue to perform duties on behalf of the lawyer that are part of the business management of a law practice, such as producing and communicating about pleadings, informing clients of upcoming hearing dates, or apprising clients of the status of their legal matters.[3] A suspended lawyer should make plans for another lawyer to assume responsibility for the work of the paralegal. Otherwise, the paralegal could be guilty of the unauthorized practice of law.

♦ THE PRACTICE OF LAW

Activity that constitutes the practice of law is established by each jurisdiction, and the definition varies from jurisdiction to jurisdiction.[4] While some jurisdictions have created precise definitions, with listed exceptions, many of the current definitions are open ended, with courts deciding on a case-by-case basis whether a new form of delivery of legal services does or does not constitute the practice of law.

In either event, there are three types of activities that are most commonly cited as being the practice of law. They are giving legal advice, representing a party in court, and preparing legal documents.[5] Almost all activities that can be considered the practice of law are encompassed within these three categories, which are discussed in the following sections. This list, however, is not all-inclusive, and courts have held that other activities also constitute the practice of law.

Giving Legal Advice

The temptation to give legal advice is a challenge that almost every paralegal encounters daily. During the span of a career, paralegals become quite familiar with certain practice areas. They learn the answers to many common client questions and may have regular interaction with clients for purposes of gathering information on behalf of the lawyer and communicating the lawyer's advice back to the client. They also may interact with third parties to request or provide information on the lawyer's behalf.

It can be very tempting to respond to a client's inquiry without first consulting the lawyer when a paralegal believes that he or she knows the answer. This is especially true when a client is kept waiting until a lawyer is available to answer the question or when a paralegal has been tasked with gathering information from a prospective client during an initial office visit or phone call. However, the response may amount to giving legal advice, so the paralegal should let the client know either that the question will be passed on to the lawyer for a response or that the client will have to discuss it with the lawyer.

Taking the above approach will not only protect the paralegal from committing the unauthorized practice of law, but it will also ensure that the client's interests are protected. The paralegal may not know the entire legal context of a matter and may, in fact, unwittingly give misinformation. Further, the lawyer is responsible for legal advice given to the client and for using the lawyer's best professional judgment in a matter. The lawyer relies on the paralegal not to compromise that responsibility.

There is an exception that precludes a communication from being the unauthorized practice of law: a response to a client's inquiry does not constitute the rendition of legal advice when the paralegal merely acts as a conduit of advice between a lawyer and a client.[6] If a paralegal does not convey any thoughts or advice of his or her own, then he or she is not giving legal advice and, therefore, not practicing law. However, paralegals delivering information pursuant to instruction and on behalf of a lawyer should always be certain to make it clear to the client that the lawyer is the source of the information.

Also to be considered is whether the advice is of a nature normally given as part of another business or transaction.[7] If someone who is not a lawyer dispenses law-related advice in furtherance of the ordinary course of his or her regular job, it may not amount to the practice of law.

For example, many bankers and financial planners regularly dispense advice that involves legal aspects of investment and tax situations. Likewise, real estate brokers routinely fill out preprinted real estate contracts on behalf of their customers as part of the sales transaction. Because all of these activities are part of the regular services provided by these professionals, they fall outside the boundaries of the legal advice test.

Representation in Court

The right to appear before a court and act on behalf of another is customarily restricted to licensed lawyers. There are many reasons offered for this restriction. First among them is that the rights and interests of the parties being represented may not be fully safeguarded when left in the hands of an untrained person.[8] It is also often suggested that the administration of justice is more efficient when conducted by lawyers since they are skilled in the rules of evidence and substantive law.

The prohibition against nonlawyers acting on another's behalf is not restricted to trial or appellate arenas. In some jurisdictions, activities such as answering docket calls and requesting continuances are also prohibited.[9] There is a split of authority as to whether a nonlawyer may represent a creditor at a creditors' meeting in bankruptcy proceedings.[10]

Paralegals should determine what actions are permissible in their jurisdiction. If the paralegal's supervising lawyer asks the paralegal to make an appearance that is prohibited to nonlawyers in the jurisdiction, the paralegal should refuse and explain why. While it is not an easy thing to take such a stance with one's employer, it is the right thing to do and protects the paralegal from actions against him or her for the unauthorized practice of law.

There are some exceptions to the rule that nonlawyers may not appear in court. The most notable exception is the right of self-representation, which exists by statute in federal courts[11] and has been held by the U.S. Supreme Court to apply in state criminal courts.[12]

The right of self-representation in state civil proceedings, though, is less concrete. Some jurisdictions allow individuals to represent themselves while others do not.[13] The U.S. Supreme Court has not decided this issue.

Another exception is the permission that nonlawyers are granted to represent individuals before certain administrative agencies. Some jurisdictions permit lay representation before specified state agencies, though the courts and legislatures of many of these jurisdictions are divided on the issue.[14] Nonlawyer representation before administrative or quasi-judicial bodies is generally not permitted when it would require the application of legal principles affecting the rights and obligations of the client.[15]

Although they have on occasion attempted to do so, states may not interfere with a layperson's right of representation before federal agencies located within their jurisdiction if such practice is permitted by federal law. For instance, a state may not prohibit nonlawyers who are registered to practice before the U.S. Patent and Trademark Office from performing tasks associated with preparing and prosecuting patent applications, even though such activities constitute the practice of law in that state.[16] Paralegals should examine each agency's policy on nonlawyer representation and consult with their supervisory lawyer before filing an appearance.

A final exception involves nonlawyer representation of corporations. This exception can seem puzzling because corporations are not individuals. Corporations are creatures of statute and are separate legal entities from the persons who form them. As such, they have no inherent right of self-representation.

Jurisdictions that permit corporations to represent themselves require them to appear through an officer or employee (lawyer or nonlawyer) and usually only when representing the corporation in a small-claims court or a court that is not of record.[17] Other jurisdictions forbid corporations to appear through nonlawyers, requiring them to be represented by a licensed lawyer.[18] Each jurisdiction has its own UPL rules and exceptions. Paralegals must therefore be fully familiar with the restrictions in their jurisdiction.[19]

Preparation of Legal Documents

Preparation of legal documents that affect the legal rights and responsibilities of others is an activity often restricted to lawyers.[20] Yet when paralegals working in a law firm prepare promissory notes, deeds, wills, contracts, and other documents, it is not considered the unauthorized practice of law. The reason lies in the supervisory role played by the lawyer, who must review the document and remain ultimately accountable for its accuracy and effectiveness.[21] This requirement for supervision is created by ABA Model Rule 5.3 regarding a lawyer's responsibility to supervise nonlawyer employees. A paralegal working for a lawyer in compliance with this rule can prepare documents without fear of UPL violations. It is the obligation of the paralegal and the lawyer to make sure the work product is reviewed by the lawyer before it is shown to a client or third party or filed with a court or agency.

The negotiation that leads to the preparation of a legal document is, however, a different matter. Thus, it has been held that it is the unauthorized practice of law when a nonlawyer employee of a law firm negotiates, on behalf of a creditor, the reaffirmation of a debt that may otherwise be dischargeable in a bankruptcy case, even though a lawyer for the creditor later reviewed the document.[22]

Case Managers

A number of reported disciplinary cases against lawyers for aiding the unauthorized practice of law have dealt with the use of nonlawyer case managers. In these instances, the case manager might use his or her own judgment without supervision from a lawyer in regard to a determination of liability; advise clients whether they have a viable claim; advise prospective clients regarding the execution of legal documents, the attorney-client contract, medical releases, and other documents;[23] and negotiate personal injury settlements on behalf of clients and in representing clients during recorded statements taken by insurance companies.[24] These cases also often involve an improper division of fees with a nonlawyer.

Other Activities

The practice of law includes a host of other activities, some of which, by statute or custom, may be performed by paralegals in certain jurisdictions. For example, in Wisconsin and Kentucky, paralegals may attend real estate closings on behalf of their employing lawyers,[25] while in South Carolina, it is impermissible for a nonlawyer to handle a closing.[26] And while in some states a paralegal may attend a deposition in place of a lawyer, New York, Oregon, and Pennsylvania forbid this practice.[27]

Unfortunately, there are few bright lines to guide paralegals through the maze of various jurisdictions' rules, case law, and ethics opinions. Before a paralegal undertakes a new task, he or she should check the rules of the jurisdiction to confirm that the activity is not the practice of law.

▶ MISREPRESENTATION OF STATUS GENERALLY

Misrepresentation of one's status is a form of UPL. The ultimate purpose of all rules of professional conduct is the protection of the public. If a client is misled to believe that a paralegal is a lawyer, the client will expect the paralegal to be able to take certain actions to advance his or her case that the paralegal may be either insufficiently knowledgeable to undertake or expressly prohibited from taking. Such misunderstandings, whether occurring innocently or as the result of deliberate deception, may result in harm to the client and damage to the reputation of the legal profession.

In order to prevent such misunderstandings from occurring, the paralegal should always disclose the fact that he or she is not a lawyer during initial contact with clients or potential clients.

CORRESPONDENCE

Because persons who receive a letter on law firm stationery may assume that the person signing the letter is a lawyer with the firm, a paralegal should always sign correspondence by indicating his or her position with the firm. Failure to do so constitutes misrepresentation of one's status, which is the unauthorized practice of law.[28] Such misrepresentation also may lead to severe economic results for the law firm, as in the case of a class action settlement related to alleged violations of the Fair Debt Collection Practices Act.[29]

While paralegals may, with proper disclosure, sign correspondence, they should only do so under the supervision of a lawyer and when the correspondence is non-substantive and not rising to the level of legal advice.[30]

NONLAWYER CONTRIBUTIONS ENCOURAGED

Although UPL prohibitions set limits on a paralegal's activities, the role of paralegals in the delivery of legal services is valuable and constantly expanding. There are many situations in which a paralegal's efforts can help lower legal costs and increase public access to legal services.

The ABA Commission on Nonlawyer Practice undertook a nationwide study of the evolving role of paralegals and other nonlawyer assistants.[31] After extensive research, numerous public hearings, and careful deliberations, the commission came to the following conclusions relating directly to nonlawyer practice:

- ▶ Increasing access to affordable assistance in law-related situations is an urgent goal of the legal profession and the states.
- ▶ Protecting the public from harm from persons providing assistance in law-related situations is also an urgent goal.
- ▶ When adequate protections for the public are in place, nonlawyers have important roles to perform in providing affordable access to justice.[32]

Though the report and its conclusions have not been adopted as ABA policy, the commission issued recommendations regarding nonlawyer involvement in the delivery of legal services. (See the sidebar "Recommendations of the ABA Commission on Nonlawyer Practice" on page 45.)

Unauthorized Practice of Law

Recommendations of the ABA Commission on Nonlawyer Practice

▼ The ABA Commission on Nonlawyer Practice developed the following recommendations:

▶ The American Bar Association; state, local, and specialty bar associations; the practicing bar; courts; law schools; and the federal and state governments should continue to develop and finance new and improved ways to provide access to justice to help the public meet its legal and law-related needs.

▶ The range of activities of traditional paralegals should be expanded, with lawyers remaining accountable for the paralegal's activities.

▶ States should consider allowing nonlawyer representation of individuals in state administrative agency proceedings. Nonlawyer representatives should be subject to the agencies' standards of practice and discipline.

▶ The American Bar Association should examine its ethics rules, policies, and standards to ensure that they promote the delivery of affordable competent services and access to justice.

▶ The activities of nonlawyers who provide assistance, advice, and representation authorized by statute, court rule, or agency regulation should be continued, subject to review by the entity under whose authority the services are performed.

▶ With regard to the activities of all other nonlawyers, states should adopt an analytical approach in assessing whether and how to regulate varied forms of nonlawyer activity that exist or are emerging in their respective jurisdictions.

Criteria for this analysis should include the risk of harm these activities present, whether consumers can evaluate providers' qualifications, and whether the net effect of regulating the activities will be a benefit to the public. The highest court in a jurisdiction should take the lead in examining specific nonlawyer activities within the jurisdiction, with the active support and participation of the bar and the public.[33]

In offering its recommendations, the commission noted the extent of nonlawyer practice at that time and the expanding forms of nonlawyer activity in the legal field.[34] The commission expressed hope that these recommendations would help jurisdictions address questions of increased nonlawyer practice and demands for access to legal services.[35]

CHAPTER SUMMARY

- [✓] Paralegals may conduct any law-related services at which they are competent, provided they do not engage in UPL.

- [✓] Every jurisdiction has one or more laws prohibiting the unauthorized practice of law; in most places, it is a misdemeanor punishable by fine or imprisonment.

- [✓] The most commonly cited types of activities involved in the definition of the practice of law are giving legal advice, representing a party in court, and preparing legal documents.

- [✓] A lawyer may delegate certain work to qualified paralegals as long as the lawyer supervises the work and retains responsibility for the work product.

- [✓] Paralegals delivering information pursuant to instruction and on behalf of a lawyer should always make it clear to the client that the lawyer is the source of the information.

- [✓] If the paralegal's supervising lawyer asks the paralegal to make an appearance that is prohibited to nonlawyers in the jurisdiction, the paralegal should refuse and explain why.

- [✓] A paralegal working under the supervision of a lawyer can prepare documents without fear of UPL violations. It is the obligation of the paralegal and the lawyer to make sure the work product is reviewed by the lawyer.

- [✓] The paralegal should disclose the fact that he or she is not a lawyer during initial contact with clients or potential clients.

♦ Notes

1. Model Rules of Prof'l Conduct R. 5.5(a) (2013).

2. In August 2003, the ABA House of Delegates adopted the Recommendation of the Task Force on the Model Definition of the Practice of Law, the first resolution of which stated that "the American Bar Association recommends that every state and territory adopt a definition of the practice of law." See Task Force on the Model Definition of the Practice of Law, ABA, http://www.americanbar.org/groups/professional_responsibility/task_force_model_definition_practice_law.html (last visited Apr. 8, 2015).

3. See In re Thonert, 693 N.E.2d 559 (Ind. 1998).

4. Model Rules of Prof'l Conduct R. 5.5 cmt. 2 (2013); see also ABA Standing Comm. on Client Prot., 2012 Survey of Unlicensed Practice of Law Committees ("'Practice of law' definitions are established by court rule in sixteen jurisdictions, by statute in fourteen, through case law in twenty-three, and through advisory opinions in three jurisdictions. Many jurisdictions have definitions in more than one resource, such as Illinois, which has practice definitions in case law, statute, and advisory opinion.").

5. Laws. Man. on Prof. Conduct (ABA/BNA) 21:8001 (July 20, 2011).

6. See generally Charles W. Wolfram, Modern Legal Ethics 836–37 (1986); see also Mich. State Bar Prof'l Ethics Comm., Informal Op. RI-349 (2010).

7. Laws. Man. on Prof. Conduct (ABA/BNA) 21:8001 (July 20, 2011); see State Bar of N.M. v. Guardian Abstract & Title Co., 575 P.2d 943 (N.M. 1978); In re Bercu, 78 N.Y.S.2d 209 (App. Div. 1948).

8. Wolfram, supra note 6, at 829.

9. Advisory Comm., Mo. State Bar Admin., Informal Op. 1 (1982).

10. See Laws. Man. on Prof. Conduct (ABA/BNA) 21:8012 (July 20, 2011).

11. See 28 U.S.C. § 1654 (1994).

12. Faretta v. California, 422 U.S. 806 (1975).

13. The following cases discuss the right of self-representation in civil matters heard in state courts: State v. Dunlap, 623 P.2d 408, 410 (Colo. 1981) (court may impose restrictions on right in order to maintain control in courtroom); Dobbins v. Dobbins, 216 S.E.2d 102, 103 (Ga. 1975) (right of self-representation guaranteed by Georgia Constitution); Ann Arbor Bank v. Weber, 61 N.W.2d 84, 86 (Mich. 1953) (right of self-representation guaranteed under Michigan Constitution); Blair v. Maynard, 324 S.E.2d 391 (W. Va. 1984) (right of self-representation in civil proceedings is fundamental right under West Virginia Constitution).

14. Laws. Man. on Prof. Conduct (ABA/BNA) 21:8008 (July 20, 2011); see Bd. of Educ. v. N.Y. State Pub. Emp't Relations Bd., 649 N.Y.S.2d 523 (App. Div. 1996); In re Burson, 909 S.W.2d 768 (Tenn. 1995).

15. Laws. Man. on Prof. Conduct (ABA/BNA) 21:8008 (July 20, 2011).

16. Sperry v. Florida, 373 U.S. 379 (1963).

17. Laws. Man. on Prof. Conduct (ABA/BNA) 21:8014 (July 20, 2011).

18. See, e.g., Greer v. Ludwick, 241 N.E.2d 4 (Ill. App. Ct. 1968).

19. The ABA Center for Professional Responsibility, in conjunction with the ABA Standing Committee on Client Protection, has published a compilation of state-by-state rules on the unauthorized practice of law. The 1994 *Survey and Related Materials on the Unauthorized Practice of Law/Nonlawyer Practice* includes a brief history of UPL, the ABA Model Rules for Advisory Opinions on the Unauthorized Practice of Law, and state-by-state survey results concerning UPL definition, enforcement, remedies, and guidelines.

20. *See, e.g.*, R.I. SUP. CT., GUIDELINES FOR USE OF LEGAL ASSISTANTS, PROVISIONAL ORDER NO. 18 (1983). *But see* ARIZ. CODE OF JUDICIAL ADMIN., pt. 7, ch. 2, § 7-208 (effective Apr. 1, 2003) (permits individuals certified pursuant to that section "to prepare or provide legal documents, without the supervision of an attorney, for an entity or member of the public who is engaging in self-representation in any legal matter").

21. ABA Comm. on Ethics & Prof'l Responsibility, Formal Op. 316 (1967). At least one court has referred to this process as the lawyer adopting the nonlawyer's work as the lawyer's own. State *ex rel.* Or. State Bar v. Lenske, 584 P.2d 759, 765 (Or. 1978).

22. *In re* Carlos, 227 B.R. 535 (Bankr. C.D. Cal. 1998).

23. *In re* Guirard, 11 So. 3d 1017 (La. 2009).

24. *In re* Garrett, 12 So. 3d 332 (La. 2009).

25. *See* Wis. Ethics Op. E-95-3 (1995) (the paralegal must be properly trained, instructed, and supervised, and the particular closing must be unlikely to involve issues requiring the presence of a lawyer); Countrywide Home Loans Inc. v. Ky. Bar Ass'n, 113 S.W.3d 105 (Ky. 2003) ("Laypersons may conduct real estate closings on behalf of other parties, but they may not answer legal questions that arise at the closing or offer any legal advice to the parties.").

26. State v. Buyers Serv. Co., 357 S.E.2d 15 (S.C. 1987).

27. Comm. on Prof'l Ethics of the Bar Ass'n of Nassau Cnty., Op. 88-53 (1988); Legal Ethics Comm. of the Or. State Bar, Op. 449 (1980); Comm. on Legal Ethics & Prof'l Responsibility of the Pa. Bar Ass'n, Op. 87-127 (1987).

28. *See, e.g.*, Fla. Bar v. Pascual, 424 So. 2d 757 (Fla. 1982)

29. *See* Fry v. Hayt, Hayt & Landau, 198 F.R.D. 461 (E.D. Pa. 2000).

30. *See* Joint Op., Advisory Comm. on Prof'l Ethics Op. 720 & Comm. on Unauthorized Practice of Law Op. 46, N.J. (Mar. 23, 2011).

31. ABA COMM'N ON NONLAWYER PRACTICE, NONLAWYER ACTIVITY IN LAW-RELATED SITUATIONS: A REPORT WITH RECOMMENDATIONS (1995) [hereinafter NONLAWYER ACTIVITY], *available at* http://www.americanbar.org/content/dam/aba/migrated/2011_build/professional_responsibility/non_lawyer_activity.authcheckdam.pdf.

32. *Id.* at 161.

33. *See* 1994 *Survey*, *supra* note 19, at 33, for a state-by-state table of permitted activities and guidelines.

34. NONLAWYER ACTIVITY, *supra* note 31, at 205.

35. *Id.*

Chapter FIVE

Competence and Diligence

- Whatever a paralegal's assignments—whether assisting governmental employers in formulating policy and regulations, helping businesspersons in meeting legal requirements, contributing to the analysis of legal matters, or performing day-to-day functions such as record keeping in a small law office—and whatever the level of supervision, the assignments always must be carried out competently and diligently.

ABA Model Rule 1.1

The drafters of the ABA Model Rules of Professional Conduct chose to give competence the most prominent place in the body of legal ethics rules. It is the very first rule, Model Rule 1.1.[1] This prominence among the rules makes sense because competence is necessary in every matter a lawyer or paralegal handles and in each step in the delivery of legal services.

Rule 1.1 makes a very straightforward statement: "A lawyer shall provide competent representation to a client."[2]

In order to adhere to this mandate, a lawyer must be able to rely upon any work done by a paralegal. A lawyer's reliance on a paralegal who performs inadequate research, fails to check the facts, or otherwise produces inferior work may result in a client receiving flawed legal advice and being harmed.

Though ABA Model Rule 1.1 does not specifically define competence, it outlines the components of competent representation: "Competent representation requires the legal knowledge, skill, thoroughness, and preparation reasonably necessary for the representation."[3] This language, though directed to lawyers, is equally applicable to the work of paralegals.

Knowledge and Skill

At the present time, there is no established measurable standard identifying the knowledge and skill a paralegal must possess in order to be considered competent. Clearly, a paralegal should understand the basic substantive concepts and relevant law in each area he or she is working in, whether it be real estate, corporations, domestic relations, or any other area.

It also is important to understand the general operation of the legal system and all procedural requirements specific to the area of one's work. For example, a lawyer will often rely upon a paralegal to "know the ropes" around the courthouse. Knowing where and how to get things done, such as the filing of court documents, can be an essential element of the paralegal's job.

A lawyer, particularly one in a small practice, also may look to a paralegal for help in regard to various aspects of practice management. The commentary to Model Rule 1.1 suggests that "a lawyer should keep abreast of changes in the law and its practice, including the benefits and risks associated with relevant technology."[4] The paralegal may be able to help in that regard.

The competent paralegal should possess the ability to identify information pertinent to a representation and to obtain that information by use of both formal and informal discovery methods. The paralegal also should be able to analyze, organize, and prepare the factual and legal data obtained to save valuable time for the lawyer.

The paralegal should be skilled at conducting the type of legal research appropriate to his or her area of work. This will require knowing the organization and structure of the law library, appropriately using library tools to conduct research, and understanding the difference between primary and secondary legal reference sources. The necessary research knowledge and skill appropriate to the area of work may take the paralegal beyond the confines of the law library. For example, if the paralegal is involved in a real estate matter, it may mean knowing how to search through books at the local recorder of deeds to uncover the chain of title to a parcel of land.

Competency, in this day and age, means familiarity and comfort with electronic research techniques. Because of the timeliness of the information available online, a paralegal who has the skills to use these research tools offers an advantage to the lawyer and client. However, given the relative ease of creating Internet sites and posting to them, when researching online, one must be particularly careful to use primary sources of information whenever possible and to confirm the accuracy of secondary sources.

The lawyer may ask the paralegal to draft correspondence or basic legal documents. The paralegal should therefore be able to write clearly and effectively. The paralegal must understand the goals, manner of and organization of documents needed in the lawyer's practice, and the style and tone necessary for correspondence to clients and others. Although the lawyer ultimately will review all documents, the paralegal should strive for perfection in the initial preparation. In this way there will be less chance of an error.

During the course of a paralegal's employment, he or she may be asked to take on new areas of responsibility, or there may be substantive or procedural changes in the area of law in which the paralegal works. Just as a lawyer would do under similar circumstances, a paralegal should respond to such developments by obtaining the requisite additional or new knowledge and skill through continuing education and study.

EC-1.1(a) of the National Federation of Paralegal Associations (NFPA) Model Code of Ethics and Professional Responsibility and Canon 6 of the National Association for Legal Assistants (NALA) Code of Ethics and Professional Responsibility provide that paralegals shall achieve competency through education in fulfilling their duty of making legal services available to clients.

When a paralegal has not yet attained sufficient knowledge or skills to handle a particular matter, it is his or her responsibility to make that fact known promptly to the supervising lawyer so that the client's interests are not jeopardized.

Thoroughness and Preparation

Professional conduct for a paralegal requires application of knowledge and utilization of formal skills in a prompt and thorough fashion. As in any business or profession, accuracy, attention to detail, efficiency, timeliness, and economy of effort are all important.

Though ABA Model Rule 1.1 does not elaborate on the meaning of "thoroughness" or "preparation," the comment to the rule states: "Competent handling of a particular matter includes inquiry into and analysis of the factual and legal elements of the problem, and use of methods and procedures meeting the standards of competent practitioners. It also includes adequate preparation."[5]

With constant pressure to work quickly and to meet difficult or demanding deadlines, a paralegal is often faced with the question of how much preparation is enough. The comment includes this word of advice: "The required attention and preparation are determined in part by what is at stake; major litigation and complex transactions ordinarily require more elaborate treatment than matters of lesser consequence."[6]

In this, as in other aspects of legal service, the paralegal is called upon to exercise judgment and to observe the spirit of the rule. When doubt exists, consulting with a supervising lawyer can help identify the appropriate amount of preparation in regard to a particular matter.

Legal Research

A lawyer has an ethical responsibility to a client to undertake a sufficient amount of research to competently represent the client in a pending matter. The paralegal will have to use his or her best judgment as to how much research is enough given the parameters of the assignment by the lawyer, but the paralegal should communicate his or her progress to the lawyer and seek guidance from the lawyer as needed to help determine whether further research is necessary.

Clearly, a failure to find available legal authority that would support the client's position could lead to unfortunate results. However, there are two reasons why it is important for the paralegal to advise the lawyer not only about supportive information that has been discovered but also about legal authority that might support the other side. First, knowing about the adverse authority will keep the lawyer from being surprised and allow the lawyer to prepare an argument as to why that authority should not be followed. Second, the ethics rules provide that "a lawyer shall not fail to disclose to the tribunal legal authority in the controlling jurisdiction known to the lawyer to be directly adverse to the position of the client and not disclosed by opposing counsel."[7] The paralegal's knowledge of the authority could easily be attributed to the lawyer.

A lawyer also has an ethical duty to charge a reasonable fee.[8] Thus, though it is important for a paralegal to be thorough when doing research, care must be taken not to do unnecessary work. For example, the paralegal should not duplicate research that may have already been done on a previous matter for the same or a different client. All that should be done is to update and cite-check the research as necessary. A lawyer who is billing a client by the hour may not bill for work product that is being reused.[9] This same logic applies to materials taken from other sources. For example, at least one court has disciplined a lawyer for plagiarizing part of a brief from a legal treatise and inflating his fees to cover the alleged time spent researching and writing the brief.[10]

To keep research costs at a minimum, a paralegal should establish a plan before beginning research. The plan should consist of a brief outline of issues to research, sources to consult, and approximate time to devote to each question. Being able to budget time for research and leave adequate time to draft the results is the mark of an experienced professional and fulfills the professional obligation to diligently represent a client. Because the time spent on research is related to the fee charged by the lawyer, issues of supervision by the lawyer (discussed more generally in Chapter 2) will apply.[11]

♦ MODEL RULE 1.3

Diligence, although addressed by a separate rule, is closely related to competence. ABA Model Rule 1.3 states that "[a] lawyer shall act with reasonable diligence and promptness in representing a client."[12]

Emphasizing the importance of diligence in the handling of legal matters, the comment to Model Rule 1.3 cautions further: "Perhaps no professional shortcoming is more widely resented than procrastination. A client's interests often can be adversely affected by the passage of time or the change of conditions; in extreme instances, as when a lawyer overlooks a statute of limitations, the client's legal position may be destroyed."[13] There are numerous reported cases of lawyers being disciplined for their failure to provide diligent representation.[14]

Moreover, as the comment states, "[e]ven when the client's interests are not affected in substance, however, unreasonable delay can cause a client needless anxiety and undermine confidence in the lawyer's trustworthiness."[15] A paralegal may be charged with the responsibility of maintaining office schedules of appointments, assignments, filing dates, and so forth.

The importance of completing tasks in a timely fashion and keeping the lawyer advised of impending deadlines cannot be overstressed: Missing a statute of limitations or filing deadline may result not only in the loss of a client but also in a malpractice suit and/or disciplinary charge against the lawyer. To help prevent this from happening, the paralegal should consult with the lawyer regarding the prioritization of work and advise the lawyer at the earliest opportunity if it appears that a heavy workload may preclude timely completion of any projects.

To prevent neglect of client matters in the event that a lawyer who is a solo practitioner dies or becomes disabled, the lawyer may need to prepare a plan that designates another competent lawyer to review client files, notify clients of the lawyer's death or disability, and determine whether there is a need for immediate protective action.[16] Some states mandate that lawyers designate such a successor, inventory, surrogate, or caretaker lawyer.[17] A paralegal, informed of the plan and knowledgeable about the office, can be a valuable resource to the successor lawyer. If the paralegal knows that no successor lawyer has been named, he or she should advise the local court so that the court can appoint one. The paralegal may not engage in activities that he or she would not be permitted to engage in if the lawyer were still available.

Testing for Competence

As noted earlier, several national organizations have attempted to enumerate the elements of paralegal competence, either through inventories of necessary knowledge and skills or through design of examinations intended to test competence, but there is no common agreement among the groups.

The American Association for Paralegal Education, for example, has adopted a compilation of "core competencies" to suggest a fundamental base of knowledge and abilities for all paralegal graduates of member schools (see Appendix D). In addition to recommending knowledge about the paralegal's role in the delivery of legal services, and about the importance of ethics and professional values, the document highlights the importance of skills related to critical thinking, organizational, communication, legal research and writing, computer, interviewing and investigation, and law office management.

Both NALA and NFPA have developed examinations to test some aspects of paralegal competence. Unlike the bar exam for lawyers, these exams are not required. No paralegal is bound to demonstrate "core competencies" or to pass either the NALA or NFPA exams in order to find a job or work as a paralegal.

NALA requires those who wish to take the Certified Paralegal (CP) exam to meet certain educational requirements. The CP exam is a five-section exam, covering communications, ethics, legal research, judgment and analytical ability, and substantive law. The substantive law section covers the American legal system and four topics to be chosen by the applicant from the following areas: administrative law, bankruptcy, business organizations, civil litigation, contracts, criminal law and procedure, estate planning and probate, family law, and real estate. There are also advanced certification exams available in a number of these areas and others.[18]

NFPA's Paralegal CORE Competency Exam was developed to assess the knowledge, skills, and ability of early-career and entry-level paralegals.[19] NFPA's Paralegal Advanced Competency Exam covers tasks that experienced paralegals routinely perform—administration of client legal matters, development of client legal matters, factual and legal research, factual and legal writing, and office administration. Ethics are included in all of the areas.[20] Educational or work experience, or certain combinations of both, also constitute requirements for taking this exam.[21]

Educational Background

All groups that have established educational standards for paralegals have concluded that the educational level and capability required be at least equivalent to that of the traditional associate of arts degree. Beyond this, however, there is disagreement as to how much of that academic work should be in legal specialty courses and whether education beyond the associate degree should be required.

Because participation in these organizations is voluntary, these criteria are not binding on paralegals.[22] Competition in the marketplace is at present the final arbiter of what preparation is necessary.

To encourage uniformity in the training of paralegals and to promote high-quality educational programming, the ABA has established certain criteria for the design of paralegal programs.[23] There are over 250 ABA-approved paralegal education programs nationwide.

The National Association of Paralegals has adopted minimum educational standards for membership in NALA. Active membership is open to individuals who meet at least one of the following requirements:

1. *successfully completed the Certified Paralegal examination of NALA*

2. *graduated from an ABA-approved program of study for paralegals*

3. *graduated from a course of study for paralegals that is institutionally accredited but not ABA approved and that requires no less than the equivalent of 60 semester hours of classroom study*

4. *graduated from a course of study for paralegals other than those set forth in 2 and 3 above, plus no less than six months of in-house training as a paralegal, whose attorney-employer attests that such person is qualified as a paralegal*

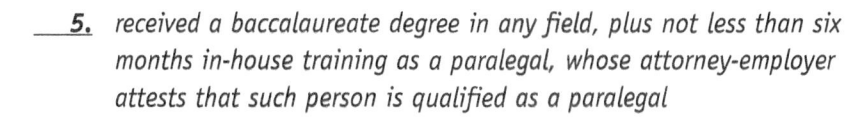

5. *received a baccalaureate degree in any field, plus not less than six months in-house training as a paralegal, whose attorney-employer attests that such person is qualified as a paralegal*

6. *has a minimum of three years of law-related experience under the supervision of an attorney, including at least six months of in-house training as a paralegal, whose attorney-employer attests that such person is qualified as a paralegal*

7. *has a minimum of two years of in-house training as a paralegal, whose attorney-employer attests that such person is qualified as a paralegal*[24]

The NFPA has also adopted recommended educational requirements for paralegals. NFPA recommends that paralegals hold either an associate or a bachelor's degree in paralegal studies (or equivalent), or an associate or a bachelor's degree (or equivalent) in any subject plus 24 semester units of legal specialty courses.[25]

♦ SUBSTANCE ABUSE AND COMPETENCY

One unfortunate, and altogether too frequent, cause for the decline of a professional's level of competence may be an addiction to alcohol or drugs. In 1988, the ABA Commission on Lawyer Assistance Programs was established with the primary goal of increasing the legal community's awareness and understanding of the signs and effects of substance abuse by lawyers. The legal profession has since initiated many programs to respond to the problem of the legal professional incapacitated by alcoholism or drug addiction, mental illness, or other causes. The ABA has issued a formal ethics opinion that discusses a lawyer's obligations with respect to a mentally impaired lawyer in the firm, recognizing that the impairment can result from alcoholism or substance abuse.[26]

An increasing number of jurisdictions have established diversionary programs through which such a lawyer is removed from active status and diverted from the disciplinary process into rehabilitative treatment programs. Some type of lawyer assistance program now exists in every state.

Law firms also are turning their attention to the personal problems of employees. In August 1990, the ABA House of Delegates adopted the Model Law Firm/Legal Department Personnel Impairment Policy and Guidelines.[27] Originally designed for use by lawyers to identify problems among their colleagues, the guidelines also can be a valuable tool for the paralegal.

Paralegals not only must ensure their own competence but also must be aware of the competence of their coworkers. In working as a team with lawyers, a paralegal is in a position to notice if there is a decline in the quality of the work of one of the team members. In order to help the individual and the firm, if the paralegal notices a problem, he or she should advise the appropriate person within the firm.

Is There a Problem?

Questions to help you assess your use of alcohol or drugs:

___ **1.** Are your associates, clients, secretary, or family alleging that your drinking or drug use is interfering with your work or home life?

___ **2.** Have you failed to show up, showed up late at the office or court because of a hangover?

___ **3.** Have you shown up at work or court under the influence of alcohol or drugs?

___ **4.** Are you drinking or using drugs during the workday?

___ **5.** Have you commingled, borrowed, or otherwise misused clients' trust or escrow funds?

___ **6.** Are you missing deadlines, neglecting to process mail, or failing to keep appointments or answer phone calls?

___ **7.** Do you ever crave a drink or a fix to steady your nerves?

___ **8.** Have you lied to cover up your drinking or use of drugs?

___ **9.** Have you consumed alcohol or used drugs before a meeting or court appearance to calm your nerves, gain courage, or improve performance?

___ **10.** Have you experienced loss of memory (blackout) after drinking or use of drugs?

___ **11.** Have you ever had [someone else] cover for you because of alcohol, drugs, or a hangover?

If you answered "yes" to two or more questions, then you owe it to yourself, your family, your clients, and your profession to call Lawyers' Assistance Program.[28]

Reprinted with permission of the Illinois Lawyers' Assistance program.

Familiarity with symptoms of abuse can assist in identifying when a person may be abusing alcohol or drugs and the extent of the problem. (See the sidebar "Is There a Problem?" above for self-directed questions that can help a paralegal or lawyer assess their use of alcohol or drugs.) If you believe that a coworker (whether a lawyer or paralegal) may have a problem, you can call your state bar association or the **ABA Commission on Lawyer Assistance Programs** to get help. The ABA Commission on Lawyer Assistance Programs website maintains a directory of local programs.

CHAPTER SUMMARY

- [✓] When a paralegal has not yet attained sufficient knowledge or skills to handle a particular matter, he or she should be sure to make that fact known promptly to the supervising lawyer so that clients' interests are not jeopardized.

- [✓] Consulting with a supervising lawyer can help identify the appropriate amount of preparation in regard to a particular matter.

- [✓] It is extremely important to complete tasks in a timely fashion and keep the lawyer advised of impending deadlines.

- [✓] It is unethical to charge a client for the time it took to do research that previously had been billed to the same or a different client.

- [✓] Paralegals not only must ensure their own competence but also must be aware of the competence of their coworkers.

- [✓] The Model Law Firm/Legal Department Personnel Impairment Policy and Guidelines can be a valuable tool for the paralegal in identifying problems among colleagues.

NOTES

1. MODEL RULES OF PROF'L CONDUCT R. 1.1 (2013).
2. *Id.*
3. *Id.*
4. *Id.* cmt. 8.
5. *Id.* cmt. 5.
6. *Id.*

7. MODEL RULES OF PROF'L CONDUCT R. 3.3(a)(2) (2013).
8. MODEL RULES OF PROF'L CONDUCT R. 1.5. Also see further discussion in Chapter 10.
9. ABA Comm. on Ethics & Prof'l Responsibility, Formal Op. 93-379 (1993).
10. *See* Iowa Supreme Ct. Bd. of Prof'l Ethics & Conduct v. Lane, 642 N.W.2d 296 (Iowa 2002).
11. *See In re* Arabia, 19 P.3d 113 (Kan. 2001) (lawyer censured for giving too little direction and supervision regarding the quantity of research and charging unreasonable fees based upon the unjustified total hours spent in researching and preparing motions).
12. MODEL RULES OF PROF'L CONDUCT R. 1.3 (2013).
13. *Id.* cmt. 3.
14. *See* ELLEN J. BENNETT, ELIZABETH J. COHEN & MARTIN WHITTAKER, ANNOTATED MODEL RULES OF PROF'L CONDUCT 46–51 (7th ed. 2011), for examples and further discussion.
15. MODEL RULES OF PROF'L CONDUCT R. 1.3 cmt. 3.
16. *See id.* cmt. 5; *see also* ABA Comm. on Ethics & Prof'l Responsibility, Formal Op. 369 (1992); MODEL RULES FOR LAWYER DISCIPLINARY ENFORCEMENT R. 28.
17. *See, e.g.*, FLA. RULES REGULATING THE BAR R. 1-3.8(e).
18. *See Certified Paralegal Examination Description,* NAT'L ASS'N LEGAL ASSISTANTS, http://nala.org/examdesc.aspx (last visited Apr. 8, 2015).
19. *See Paralegal Certification—Paralegal CORE Competency Exam and Credentialing,* NAT'L FED'N PARALEGAL ASS'NS, http://www.paralegals.org/default.asp?page=18 (last updated Mar. 5, 2015).
20. *See About the Paralegal Advanced Competency Exam (PACE),* NAT'L FED'N PARALEGAL ASS'NS, http://www.paralegals.org/default.asp?page=20.
21. *See About the Paralegal Advanced Competency Exam (PACE),* NAT'L FED'N PARALEGAL ASS'NS, http://www.paralegals.org/default.asp?page=89.
22. For further information regarding these criteria, visit the organizations' websites at http://nala.org/Default.aspx and http://www.paralegals.org.
23. ABA GUIDELINES FOR THE APPROVAL OF PARALEGAL EDUCATION PROGRAMS (effective as amended Sept. 1, 2013), *available at* http://www.americanbar.org/content/dam/aba/administrative/paralegals/ls_prlgs_2013_paralegal_guidelines.authcheckdam.pdf. Approved programs undergo the full approval process every seven years.
24. *See Qualifications,* NAT'L ASS'N LEGAL ASSISTANTS, http://nala.org/qualifications.aspx (last visited Apr. 8, 2015).
25. Nat'l Fed'n of Paralegal Ass'n, Res. 92-M3 (1992).
26. ABA Comm. on Ethics & Prof'l Responsibility, Formal Op. 429 (2003).

27. *See* ABA Model Law Firm/Legal Department Personnel Impairment Policy and Guidelines, adopted August 1990.

28. *Alcohol and Drug Abuse*, ILL. LAWS. ASSISTANCE PROGRAM, http://illinoislap.org/alcohol-and-drug-abuse (last visited Apr. 8, 2015); see Directory of Lawyer Assistance Programs, ABA, http://www.americanbar.org/groups/lawyer_assistance/resources/lap_programs_by_state.html (last visited Apr. 8, 2015).

Chapter SIX

Confidentiality

◆ The duty to keep client information confidential is one of the fundamental principles of the client-lawyer relationship. This cornerstone of legal representation enables a client to speak freely without fear that embarrassing or legally damaging information will be revealed. This, in turn, enables the lawyer to provide the client with the most informed and effective assistance possible.[1] The client's full disclosure is necessary before the lawyer can offer sound legal advice.

The principle of confidentiality is found in two related bodies of law, the rules of legal ethics and the rule of attorney-client privilege. Though the principal focus of this chapter is on the ethical rule of confidentiality, there are frequent references to the attorney-client privilege and its related work product doctrine, as those duties and the rule of confidentiality may be affected by the same conduct of the lawyer and paralegal.

The duty to maintain client confidences is imposed not only upon the lawyer but also upon the other law firm personnel as agents of the lawyer. This extension recognizes that the effectiveness of lawyers depends upon their ability to rely on the assistance of other law firm personnel.

The Paralegal and Confidentiality

Paralegals can be guided initially by two simple precepts regarding confidentiality: they should treat all client information as confidential, and they should not discuss client matters with anyone other than the lawyers and other staff who are working on the matter. Even discussing the matter with lawyers in the firm who are not involved with the matter may create problems if, for example, those lawyers are supposed to be screened from that matter (see discussion in Chapter 7). Breach of the duty of confidentiality can have serious consequences for both the client and the law firm.

EC-1.5(a) through (f) of the NFPA Model Code of Ethics and Professional Responsibility address a paralegal's obligation to preserve all confidential information provided by the client or acquired from other sources before, during, or after the course of the professional relationship. EC-1.5(d) provides that confidential information may be revealed only after full disclosure and with the client's written consent, when required by law or court order, or when necessary to prevent the client from committing an act that could result in death or serious bodily harm.

The Paralegal and Privilege

The attorney-client privilege covers information given by the client for the purpose of securing legal advice and may only be invoked to exclude confidential communications between lawyers and clients from evidence at trial and other judicial proceedings. Initial consultations are covered and communications are privileged even if the prospective client does not hire the lawyer or if the lawyer declines the representation.

The attorney-client privilege extends to paralegals and other employees of the lawyer who receive confidential information.[2] The communications to the paralegal, however, are entitled to protection only if the paralegal is performing a legal function. So, for example, it has been held that a criminal defendant's conversations with a friend who acted as a paralegal did not deserve attorney-client privilege protection.[3]

The related work product doctrine also applies to judicial proceedings and protects from discovery materials prepared by a lawyer in anticipation of litigation. Accordingly, papers developing trial strategy, notes revealing thoughts of the lawyer, and the like are protected from disclosure in the judicial process. Any similar materials prepared by the lawyer's paralegal are also protected.[4]

Effect of Disclosure on Attorney-Client Privilege

Failure to maintain a client's confidences can mean the loss of privilege regarding that information. As noted above, revelation of privileged information may be damaging to a client's case. The authority to waive the attorney-client privilege (and disclose the information) belongs only to the client. Canon 7 of the NALA Code of Ethics and Professional Responsibility states that it is unethical for a paralegal to violate any statute controlling privileged communications.

Lawyers or paralegals, however, may inadvertently waive the privilege if they share the information with a third person to whom the privilege does not extend, remove incriminating evidence from its original position, or divulge secrets to a court under a mistaken belief that disclosure is required. Waiver of the privilege means that the information can be admitted into evidence against the client at trial. Additionally, the lawyer may be subject to discipline for breaching the related ethical duty of confidentiality.

Inadvertent disclosure often arises in discovery proceedings. As a paralegal may be asked to help gather documents for production, it is important that the paralegal pay close attention to the nature of the documents being assembled and consult the lawyer if there is any uncertainty about whether a particular document should be held back as privileged. This is done through the separation and flagging of questionable documents and the creation of a privilege log. In matters where thousands of documents are involved, the lawyer may not be able to review all the documents and is permitted to rely upon the paralegal's help to perform this screening function.[5]

◆ ETHICAL DUTY OF CONFIDENTIALITY

Whereas the attorney-client privilege covers only information given by the client for the purpose of securing legal advice and may only be invoked to exclude confidential communications between lawyers and clients from evidence at trial and other judicial proceedings, the duty of confidentiality protects all information received by a lawyer in the course of representing a client, regardless of the source, and prevents disclosure of the information in any setting.[6] As with the privilege, the protection applies to information received from a prospective client, even if the lawyer does not take on the representation.

The ABA Model Rules of Professional Conduct address the protection of information relating to the representation of a client in a series of related rules. Model Rule 1.6 is the general rule regarding confidentiality of information. Other rules address conflicts of interest and imputed disqualification, subjects often implicated when a confidentiality problem arises. Still other rules govern when a lawyer may or must reveal confidential communications.

▶ INFORMATION RELATING TO REPRESENTATION

Model Rule 1.6 prohibits a lawyer, with certain exceptions, from revealing "information relating to the representation of a client." This includes everything the client tells the lawyer, whether directly to the lawyer or through paralegals and other people working with the lawyer. It also includes everything the lawyer learns, no matter the source, while investigating and developing the facts of a case.

A lawyer may be deemed to have acquired protected information even when the lawyer is not yet acting on behalf of a client. For example, protected information can include information obtained during an interview with a prospective client, even if he or she does not retain the lawyer and the lawyer performs no legal services for the prospective client.[7] And it is important to know that, even if the original contact is with the paralegal, and not with the lawyer, confidentiality protections may attach that could affect the lawyer's ability to represent another client whose interests are adverse to the prospective client.[8] Thus it is important in such a situation that the paralegal limit the amount of confidential information obtained to only that information necessary to perform a conflicts analysis.[9]

In this regard, the confidentiality rule parallels the attorney-client privilege.[10] This information may create a conflict of interest that would disqualify a lawyer from representing someone with an adverse claim; however, if the prospective client consults the lawyer in an effort to disqualify the lawyer or for some purpose other than seeking legal representation, the information disclosed does not relate to representation and is not protected.[11]

Thus, when a prospective client interviews several lawyers before retaining one, the presumption that the information disclosed is confidential may be rebuttable. Lawyer shopping does not always create a client-lawyer relationship. In 2002, the ABA adopted a new rule of professional conduct on duties to prospective clients, which provides guidance on this issue.[12]

Once a representation is undertaken, the lawyer's duty of confidentiality continues indefinitely.[13] Regardless of whether the case is concluded or the client discharges the lawyer, the lawyer must not reveal the former client's confidences.

▶ SHARING CONFIDENCES IN THE WORKPLACE

Lawyers are generally permitted to share information relating to a client with other members of their law firm, unless the client instructs the lawyer otherwise.[14] However, when a lawyer within the firm is being screened pursuant to a conflict of interest, that lawyer must not receive any information regarding the matter from which he or she is being screened. (See Chapter 7 for a discussion of screening measures.)

Generally, courts presume that what one lawyer knows will be shared with coworkers because lawyers in a firm share responsibility for their cases. Whether lawyers practice as partners or in an employer-employee relationship, the presumption is that confidences are shared if lawyers practice in some form of affiliation.[15] The presumption, however, does not extend to those outside the firm, not even to the lawyer's spouse.[16] Lawyers are presumed to uphold the duty of confidentiality by not discussing the client's private matters with any third party.

Even lawyers who do not practice in a conventional firm environment may be presumed to share client confidences. If unaffiliated lawyers share office space, or if information about a lawyer's client is available to other lawyers or their staff, the lawyers may be considered members of a single firm for conflicts of interest purposes,[17] and the disqualification of one lawyer may be imputed to the other lawyers sharing the space. The determination of whether lawyers should be considered a firm is fact based and is made on a case-by-case basis. (See Chapter 7 for a more complete discussion of conflicts of interest.)

Lawyers and paralegals must be extremely careful when discussing a client's case. For example, a lawyer can violate the client's confidences by including a business associate who is not a lawyer in a client conference.[18] On the other hand, a lawyer does not necessarily violate the duty by using an outside data processing facility to store client information, provided that the lawyer takes all reasonable steps to ensure that the confidentiality of the information is maintained.[19]

♦ TYPES OF INFORMATION

There are several different types of information. A closer look at these will reveal how the courts and the ABA Model Rules address each in relation to the issue of confidentiality.

Identity

The identity of a client and information relating to the identity of a client, such as location, address, and telephone number, are not protected by the attorney-client privilege.[20] If a client requests that such information be kept secret, however, it will be protected by the duty of confidentiality.[21]

A client's personal information may be considered confidential in other circumstances as well, such as when revelation of the information would embarrass the client or when it relates to a client's past criminal activity.[22] For example, if the client's whereabouts are unknown and the client is a fugitive, then the information is confidential and the lawyer may not reveal it.

On the other hand, the lawyer must be careful not to cross the line between protecting client confidences and participating in the client's criminal activity. If a client has been indicted on a criminal charge, the lawyer may keep silent about the client's location but may not hide the client or provide shelter.[23]

Fee Information

Generally, payment of fees, including the amount to be paid, the payment arrangements, and the person who will pay, is not considered confidential information. Courts have carved out an exception to this general rule when disclosure will provide the final piece of information needed to connect the client with a crime.[24]

Criminal Evidence

As with the whereabouts of a client who is a fugitive, knowledge or possession of the "fruit or instrumentality" (results or means of committing) of a crime implicates two principles: confidentiality of client information and the prohibition against assisting a crime.

The prohibition against assisting a crime is a reason the ABA amended Model Rule 1.6 in 2003 to allow a lawyer to reveal otherwise confidential information under certain circumstances when the client has used or is using the lawyer's services in furtherance of a crime or fraud.

Although, absent the special circumstances outlined in Model Rule 1.6, a lawyer must keep silent about a client's past crimes, he or she may not hide the fruits and instrumentalities of past crimes.[25] The following principles have emerged from the various cases on the subject. Incriminating information given by a client to a lawyer, such as the location of a murder weapon or the proceeds of a crime, is protected by the attorney-client privilege; the physical evidence itself (the gun or money) is subject to disclosure.[26] The lawyer may even have an affirmative obligation to turn over to the prosecution any evidence unearthed during preparation for trial,[27] even if the client gave the evidence to the lawyer.[28]

A key issue in the analysis of the confidentiality of evidence is whether the lawyer leaves the evidence in its original position. If the lawyer knows of incriminating evidence and leaves it where it is originally found, the evidence will be protected from disclosure. Once the lawyer removes the evidence to inspect it or test it, or for any other reason, the evidence loses the protection of the privilege, and the lawyer can be compelled to turn it over.[29] The paralegal should be careful not to handle such evidence unless specifically directed to do so by the supervising lawyer.

♦ When the Client Is a Corporation

Because a business organization cannot speak for itself, lawyers provide legal advice to a corporation or partnership based on the information given to the lawyer by those who are the officers or partners of the organization. It also is natural in the course of a day for an organization's employees to talk to the lawyer about matters that are not related to corporate or partnership representation. What, then, must the lawyer keep confidential?

The U.S. Supreme Court case of *Upjohn Co. v. United States* and the comment to ABA Model Rule 1.13 make it clear that when an organization's director, officer, or employee communicates with a lawyer in that person's capacity as a representative of the organization, the communication "relates to the representation" and is confidential.[30]

It is important to note that although confidential information may be obtained from any of the above-named organizational constituents, some of them may not be entitled to receipt of confidential information on behalf of the entity. The paralegal should always defer to the lawyer's judgment in this regard and not share information with someone at the organizational client unless the lawyer has stated specifically that it is permissible to do so.

♦ Authorized and Unauthorized Disclosures

The ABA Model Rules set forth several exceptions to a lawyer's duty of confidentiality. The first is that a lawyer may reveal information relating to a representation if the client authorizes the revelation. Authorization can be express or implied. An express authorization must be accompanied by informed consent; that is, the client must approve after consulting with the lawyer about what the lawyer is doing and what information will be disclosed. Authorization may be implied if necessary to effect the representation or if joint representation is involved.

Prevention of Bodily Harm, Crime, or Fraud

Prior to 2003, Model Rule 1.6(b)(1) permitted disclosure of confidential information "to prevent the client from committing a criminal act that the lawyer believes is likely to result in imminent death or substantial bodily harm." This provision proved to be one of the most controversial of the ABA's ethics rules. In 2003, the criminality requirement was deleted from Model Rule 1.6(b)(1), and the rule was broadened to permit disclosure "to prevent reasonably certain death or substantial bodily harm." Such disclosure is permitted but not required. On the other hand, South Carolina, for example, has deleted the "death and serious bodily harm" requirement from its version of Rule 1.6, permitting a lawyer to reveal information necessary to prevent any criminal act.[31] And Virginia *requires*, after certain steps to dissuade the client, disclosure of a client's intention to commit any crime and the information necessary to prevent the crime.[32]

In addition, in 2003, the current Model Rule 1.6(b)(2) was added. This provision permits a lawyer to disclose confidential information "to prevent the client from committing a crime or fraud that is reasonably certain to result in substantial injury to the financial interests or property of another and in furtherance of which the client has used or is using the lawyer's services." The states have adopted various permutations. For example, New Jersey *requires* a lawyer to reveal confidential information to prevent the client "from committing a criminal, illegal or fraudulent act that the lawyer reasonably believes is likely to result in . . . substantial injury to the financial interest or property of another."[33]

Past Acts

Current ABA Model Rule 1.6(b)(3), adopted in 2003, permits a lawyer to disclose confidential information in order to "prevent, mitigate or rectify substantial injury to the financial interests or property of another that . . . has resulted from the client's commission of a crime or fraud in furtherance of which the client has used the lawyer's services." Quite a few states have the same or a similar provision in their professional conduct codes.

The justification for this type of disclosure is well expressed in the phrase generally used to describe it: rectification of criminal or fraudulent acts. The purpose is to allow lawyers to reveal whatever information an injured party needs in order to rectify past harm. The important thing to remember in regard to this provision of the Model Rules and in regard to Rule 1.6(b)(2) is that the client must have used the lawyer's services in order for the disclosure to be permissible.

Compliance with the Ethics Rules

A lawyer may reveal information relating to a representation to a lawyer outside the firm from whom legal advice is being sought regarding compliance with the rules of professional conduct.

Establishment of Claim or Self-Defense

The ABA Model Rules also allow a lawyer to reveal confidential information if necessary to establish (1) a claim against the client or (2) a defense to an accusation of criminal or unethical conduct arising out of the representation.

This exception most often occurs when a lawyer tries to collect a fee or defend against a malpractice claim by the client. The disclosure must be made only to the extent necessary to establish the claim or defense, and it must be limited to those people who need the information.

Change of Employment

In 2012, the ABA Model Rules were amended to provide a firmer basis for and guidance related to the limitations on disclosures made by lawyers to detect and resolve conflicts arising from a change of employment. Although some disclosure of information regarding the representation of a client is permitted, the lawyer must not reveal information that would compromise the attorney-client privilege or otherwise prejudice the client.

A paralegal changing employment should keep the same considerations in mind. (See Chapter 7 on conflicts for additional discussion of issues related to paralegals switching firms.)

Client Perjury

Although ABA Model Rule 1.6 does not specifically permit disclosure of client perjury as an exception to the confidentiality rule, other rules may require disclosure. Perjury is a fraud on the courts, and ABA Model Rule 3.3, concerning candor toward tribunals, requires a lawyer to disclose to a court material facts necessary to avoid assisting a criminal or fraudulent act, even if the information is otherwise confidential.[34] The ABA Standing

Committee on Ethics and Professional Responsibility has interpreted Model Rule 3.3 to require that if a lawyer discovers a client's perjury before the close of the proceedings, the lawyer must inform the court of the perjury. If the lawyer learns that the client intends to commit perjury and the lawyer cannot prevent the client from testifying falsely, then the lawyer must disclose to the court the client's intention to commit perjury.[35]

♦ WITHDRAWAL FROM REPRESENTATION

Whether or not the circumstances are such that Model Rule 1.6 permits a lawyer to reveal client information, Model Rule 1.16 permits the lawyer to withdraw from representation "if the client has used the lawyer's services to perpetrate a crime or fraud" or the "client persists in a course of action involving the lawyer's services that the lawyer reasonably believes is criminal or fraudulent." Again, note that the lawyer's services must have been involved. Furthermore, the rule requires withdrawal if "the representation will result in violation of the Rules of Professional Conduct or other law."

The lawyer is not required to withdraw if the crime or fraud is complete, but the lawyer must withdraw if the crime or fraud is occurring and the client is using the lawyer's services to carry it out. Lawyers must use their professional judgment to determine whether a fraud is continuing. As with permissive withdrawal, the lawyer may not reveal any of the former client's confidences except to prevent aiding the ongoing fraud. A court ordinarily should accept a "lawyer's statement that professional considerations require termination of the representation" so that the lawyer can maintain confidentiality.[36]

♦ THE PARALEGAL AND CONFIDENTIAL INFORMATION

For paralegals, the issue of whether information is confidential usually arises in two situations: when discussing a case outside the firm with a friend or relative and when responding to discovery requests.

Discussing Client Matters

Discussing a client's case with a friend or relative may be tempting. Sometimes, a paralegal just wants a second opinion on an assignment. Discussing cases may seem harmless if the names of the parties are changed or shielded. However, talking about cases, even innocently, is a breach of client confidentiality. Client information must never be discussed outside the firm.

This is an absolute duty, easily fulfilled simply by the paralegal remaining silent. One never knows who may be acquainted with a client or with someone connected with a case or who may overhear a conversation. Concealing names will not be enough to protect confidential information if the listener (or someone else) can put all the pieces together. Revealing the information could result in a lost case, a malpractice suit, and a disciplinary action against the lawyer. It is important to remember that the prohibition against discussing client matters outside the firm extends not only to information but also to deliberations within the firm as to how the firm intends to handle the representation.

Office Maintenance and Sharing

It is also important to be careful when discussing confidential matters at the office. In addition to the diligence that one must pay to any screening mechanisms as described in Chapter 7, the paralegal should not discuss client matters in front of visitors, let visitors walk around the office unattended, or leave confidential paperwork lying around in open view.

These considerations gain added significance when some type of office-sharing arrangement is involved. Many small law firms share office space with other firms or solo practitioners; they may also share paralegals. In such situations, special precautions must be taken to prevent sharing of confidential information about clients who have conflicting interests. It will be much easier to do so if the practices of the sharing firms are such that their clients are unlikely to have adverse interests.[37] The paralegal who is offered a position in an office-sharing situation should discuss the potential problems and necessary precautions at the time of the offer.

Complying with Discovery Requests

Responding to discovery requests is a standard paralegal task. Some firms tag confidential files so employees know to take special caution with them. A paralegal should become familiar with systems designed to label confidential documents.

When responding to a discovery request, a paralegal should look over each piece of paper that will be sent to opposing counsel and determine if it contains any client confidences. If any papers do, the paralegal should discuss with the supervising lawyer the need to redact the confidential information and then make whatever changes are necessary to remove the information from versions being prepared for delivery to the opposing side. Once that is accomplished, the paralegal still should not send out the documents until the supervising lawyer has reviewed them to ensure that no confidential information remains.

Even inadvertent disclosure can destroy the attorney-client privilege. Revelation of just one piece of privileged information can open the door to a request for all of the client's confidential information.

The Use of Technology

There has been a great deal of discussion about transmission of confidential information via e-mail or cell phone. ABA Model Rule 1.6 states that lawyers must "make reasonable efforts to prevent the inadvertent or unauthorized disclosure of, or unauthorized access to, information relating to the representation of a client." A North Carolina ethics opinion pointed out that the obligation of confidentiality does not require that a lawyer use only infallibly secure methods of communication.[38] Therefore, making calls with a cellular phone is permissible, but reasonable care should be used if there is any cause to believe that interception of the confidential communication is an issue.

Some law firms have established direct e-mail links with clients in part to avoid the risk of interception. The ABA issued a formal opinion that approved transmission of information relating to the representation of a client via unencrypted e-mail sent over the Internet.[39] However, the opinion cautioned that a lawyer should consult with a client and follow the client's instructions as to the mode of transmitting highly sensitive information. Therefore, it is important that the paralegal be aware of any such client instructions before transmitting confidential information via e-mail.

Paralegals should be careful to follow their supervising lawyer's instructions as to scrubbing electronic documents or creating versions that do not contain embedded information. Several state ethics opinions have stated that lawyers must use reasonable care to ensure that metadata that contain confidential information are not disclosed to a third party.[40]

Receiving Inadvertent Disclosures

Courts are divided on how lawyers should handle the receipt of confidential information that has been mistakenly delivered to them. Some courts enforce the attorney-client privilege if the opposing party asserts that disclosure was inadvertent,[41] but others permit the lawyer to use the information on the theory that, however inadvertent, the privilege is destroyed.[42]

ABA Model Rule 4.4(b) states that "[a] lawyer who receives a document or electronically stored information relating to the representation of the lawyer's client and knows or reasonably should know that the document or electronically stored information was inadvertently sent shall promptly notify the sender." The comment to the Model Rule makes clear that "[a] document or electronically stored information is inadvertently sent when it is accidentally transmitted, such as when an email or letter is misaddressed or a document or electronically stored information is accidentally included with information that was intentionally transmitted."

The Model Rules do not prohibit the receiving lawyer from looking at an opposing party's metadata, whether or not the document has been inadvertently sent, though some state ethics opinions have reached the opposite conclusion.

If paralegals receive information that appears to be confidential, whether through the mail or via messenger service, fax, or e-mail, they should consult with their supervising lawyer to determine what course to take. Though the return of inadvertently delivered confidential information is not required by most states, there is some authority supporting such action.[43] And if paralegals inadvertently send confidential information, they should immediately advise their supervising lawyer of the mistake.

Multiple Clients in the Same or Related Matters

It is not unusual for law firms to represent more than one client in the same or related matters. As pointed out in ABA Ethics Opinion 08-450, "the obligation of confidentiality to each [client] sometimes may conflict with the obligation of disclosure to each." Thus, to be safe, when multiple clients are involved, a paralegal should consult with the lawyer handling the matter before sharing any information relating to the representation with any of the clients.

CHAPTER SUMMARY

- ☑ The duty to maintain client confidences is imposed upon all law firm personnel.

- ☑ Anything a paralegal hears or learns as a result of his or her employment is strictly confidential.

- ☑ Office matters should not be discussed with anyone other than the client whose matter is involved or other employees of the firm known to be working on the matter (and then subject to any limitations required by the conflicts rules discussed in Chapter 7).

- ☑ The prohibition against discussing client matters outside the firm extends not only to information but also to deliberations within the firm as to how the firm intends to handle the representation.

- ☑ Information obtained from a prospective client is protected even if the prospective client does not hire the lawyer.

- ☑ If the client is an organization, the paralegal should not share information with someone at the client organization unless the lawyer has stated specifically that it is permissible to do so.

- ☑ If a paralegal mistakenly receives information that appears to be confidential, whether through the mail or via fax or e-mail, he or she should consult with the supervising lawyer to determine what course to take.

- ☑ A paralegal should not handle evidence related to a criminal matter absent specific direction from the supervising lawyer.

♦ NOTES

1. Fisher v. United States, 425 U.S. 391 (1976).
2. Pennsylvania v. Mrozek, 657 A.2d 997 (Pa. 1995); Samaritan Found. v. Superior Court, 844 P.2d 593 (Ariz. 1993).
3. Volrie v. State, No. 13 05 667 CR, 2007 Tex. App. LEXIS 6574 (Aug. 16, 2007) (unpublished opinion).
4. *See* Ins. Co. of N. Am. v. Superior Court, 166 Cal. Rptr. 880, 888 (Ct. App. 1980); FED. R. CIV. P. 26(b)(3).
5. *See, e.g.*, Aramony v. United Way of Am., 969 F. Supp. 226 (S.D.N.Y. 1997).
6. ELLEN J. BENNETT, ELIZABETH J. COHEN & HELEN GUNNARSSON, ANNOTATED MODEL RULES OF PROF'L CONDUCT 96 (8th ed. 2015).
7. MODEL RULES OF PROF'L CONDUCT R. 1.18 (2013); ABA Comm. on Ethics & Prof'l Responsibility, Formal Op. 358 (1990).
8. Va. State Bar Legal Ethics Op. 1832 (2007).
9. *Id.*
10. *See* Arthur Garwin, *Confidentiality and Its Relationship to the Attorney-Client Privilege, in* ATTORNEY-CLIENT PRIVILEGE IN CIVIL LITIGATION (6th ed., ABA 2015).
11. ABA Comm. on Ethics & Prof'l Responsibility, Formal Op. 358 (1990).
12. MODEL RULES OF PROF'L CONDUCT R. 1.18 (2013).
13. MODEL RULES OF PROF'L CONDUCT R. 1.6 cmt. 18 (2013).
14. *Id.* cmt. 5.
15. Skokie Gold Standard Liquors, Inc. v. Joseph E. Seagram & Sons, Inc., 452 N.E.2d 804 (Ill. App. Ct. 1983).
16. *See, e.g.*, Non-punitive Segregation Inmates v. Kelly, 589 F. Supp. 1330 (E.D. Pa. 1984) (courts will not presume lawyer discloses confidences to close friends or spouse); ABA Comm. on Ethics & Prof'l Responsibility, Formal Op. 340 (1975).
17. BENNETT, COHEN & GUNNARSSON, *supra* note 6, at 182.
18. *In re* Agnew, 311 N.W.2d 869 (Minn. 1981).
19. ABA Comm. on Ethics & Prof'l Responsibility, Informal Op. 1364 (1976).
20. *In re* Grand Jury Proceedings, 680 F.2d 1026 (5th Cir. 1982); ABA Comm. on Ethics & Prof'l Responsibility, Informal Op. 1411 (1978).
21. *In re* Kozlov, 398 A.2d 882 (N.J. 1979); Brennan v. Brennan, 422 A.2d 510 (Pa. Super. Ct. 1980).
22. *In re* Stolar, 397 F. Supp. 520 (S.D.N.Y. 1975); *In re* Burns, 536 N.E.2d 1206 (Ct. Com. Pl. 1988); ABA Comm. on Ethics & Prof'l Responsibility, Informal Op. 1287 (1974).
23. *In re* DeMassa, 60 U.S.L.W. 2385 (Cal. Bar Ct. 1991).
24. Baird v. Koerner, 279 F.2d 623 (9th Cir. 1960). This is known as the "last link" theory.

25. *In re* Ryder, 263 F. Supp. 360 (E.D. Va. 1967), *aff'd*, 381 F.2d 713 (4th Cir. 1967) (lawyer who stored gun and apparent robbery proceeds in lawyer's safe deposit box suspended for 18 months).

26. Peter A. Joy & Kevin C. McMunigal, *Incriminating Evidence—Too Hot to Handle?*, 24 CRIM. JUST. 42 (2009).

27. Pennsylvania v. Stenhach, 514 A.2d 114 (Pa. Super. Ct. 1986).

28. California v. Superior Court, 237 Cal. Rptr. 158 (Ct. App. 1987).

29. *See* California v. Meredith, 631 P.2d 46, 54 (Cal. 1981) ("If defense counsel leaves the evidence where he discovers it, his observations derived from privileged communications are insulated from revelation. If, however, counsel chooses to remove evidence to examine or test it, the original location and condition of that evidence loses the protection of the privilege.").

30. Upjohn Co. v. United States, 449 U.S. 383 (1981); MODEL RULES OF PROF'L CONDUCT R. 1.13 cmt. 2 (2013).

31. RULE 407, SCACR, RULES OF PROF'L CONDUCT R. 1.6.

32. VA. RULES OF PROF'L CONDUCT R. 1.6(c)(1).

33. N.J. RULES OF PROF'L CONDUCT R. 1.6.

34. MODEL RULES OF PROF'L CONDUCT R. 3.3 (2013).

35. ABA Comm. on Ethics & Prof'l Responsibility, Formal Op. 353 (1987).

36. MODEL RULES OF PROF'L CONDUCT R. 1.16 cmt. 3 (2013); *see also* MODEL RULES OF PROF'L CONDUCT R. 3.3 cmt. 15.

37. *See* Ky. Bar Ass'n Op. E-406 (1998).

38. N.C. STATE BAR, RULES OF PROF'L CONDUCT R. 215 (1995).

39. ABA Comm. on Ethics & Prof'l Responsibility, Formal Op. 413 (1999).

40. *See, e.g.*, Colo. Op. 119 (May 17, 2008).

41. Mendenhall v. Barber-Greene Co., 531 F. Supp. 951 (N.D. Ill. 1982).

42. *See, e.g., In re* Grand Jury Investigation of Ocean Transp., 604 F.2d 672 (D.C. Cir. 1979) (accidental delivery of privileged documents to grand jury destroyed privilege); *see also* CHARLES W. WOLFRAM, MODERN LEGAL ETHICS 272–73 (1986).

43. Berg Elec., Inc. v. Molex, Inc., 875 F. Supp. 261 (D. Del. 1995); Richards v. Jain, 168 F. Supp. 2d 1195 (W.D. Wash. 2001) (attorney who receives privileged documents has ethical duty, upon notice of privileged nature of the documents, to cease review of the documents, notify privilege holder, and return documents; failure to abide by these rules is grounds for disqualification).

Chapter SEVEN

Conflicts of Interest

- When a client hires a lawyer, the client has a right to expect that his or her best interests will be paramount for the lawyer and the lawyer's team working on the matter. They owe the client that duty. If interests adverse to the client's interests compromise the judgment of the lawyer or the legal team, the client may suffer damage. Such situations may arise when a lawyer's duty to a client conflicts with a duty to another current, prospective, or former client. The duties most often involved are the duty of loyalty and the duty to maintain client confidences. There also may be instances when a client's interests are not compatible with the lawyer's personal interests.

These situations are further complicated by the movement of lawyers and paralegals between firms, because they may have had access to confidential client information at the first firm that impacts a client of the second firm. In addition, as law firms merge or otherwise increase in size, and the numbers of lawyers, paralegals, and past and present clients grow, there is an ever greater likelihood that prospective clients will have interests adverse to those of other current or former clients.

The network of conflict rules is among the most complicated of all the ethics rules. Many of the issues regarding conflicts of interest will require decisions by the firm's lawyers that will not involve the paralegal. However, the paralegal may have responsibilities in connection with the firm's conflict-checking system and thus will need a basic understanding of the issues. In addition, some of the ethics rules pertaining to conflicts of interest do involve types of conduct in which a paralegal might participate and about which the paralegal must be aware. The following is a brief outline of issues related to conflicts of interest.

◆ GENERAL CONSIDERATIONS

Loyalty is the foundation of the client-lawyer relationship.[1] It is crucial that the paralegal support the lawyer in avoiding conflicts of interest, and so the paralegal must be aware of the governing principles. An impermissible conflict of interest may exist before representation is undertaken that would suggest that the lawyer decline representation of a client.[2] However, not all potential conflicts of interest preclude representation. Under certain circumstances, a client who is fully informed of a potential conflict of interest may consent to the representation.[3] In general, courts interpreting the conflict of interest rules have attempted to balance the lawyer's duty of loyalty to the client, the economic interests of the lawyer, and the public's interest in the availability of legal services.

◆ DIRECTLY ADVERSE REPRESENTATION

ABA Model Rule 1.7 (Conflict of Interest: Current Clients) prohibits a lawyer from representing both the plaintiff and the defendant in a single action. It also prohibits a lawyer from representing a client in a matter and simultaneously opposing that client in another matter, even if those matters are unrelated.

For example, it would be a violation of Model Rule 1.7 for a lawyer to represent the wife in a contested divorce case and simultaneously represent the husband in a (seemingly) unrelated workers' compensation case.[4] This is because the lawyer owes an absolute duty of loyalty to the client. It is presumed that a lawyer will not be able to represent the client vigorously when the lawyer has an adversarial relationship to that client in another matter.[5]

The existence of a *potential* conflict does not necessarily preclude representation. When faced with a potential conflict, the lawyer must consider the likelihood that the conflict will develop and that it would materially interfere with the lawyer's independent judgment.[6]

One such situation is the representation of multiple parties that are nominally on the same side in a litigation matter. Although a lawyer may represent clients having similar interests if the risk of an adverse interest arising is minimal and if all clients consent after being told of the potential problems, in criminal cases the possibility of conflicting interests in representing multiple defendants is so grave that, as a general rule, lawyers traditionally have declined to represent more than one codefendant.[7]

◆ ISSUE CONFLICTS

When a lawyer is asked to advocate a position on behalf of one client that is directly contrary to the position of another of the law firm's clients, the lawyer may be required to refuse the second representation or (if otherwise permissible) withdraw from the first representation. Model Rule 1.7 would prevent a law firm from concurrently representing clients whose matters would require it to argue directly contrary positions in the same jurisdiction, unless neither case is likely to be harmful to the other.[8]

This situation requires each client to give informed consent. Factors taken into consideration in determining whether the risk of harm is great enough to require client consent include where the cases are pending, whether the issue is substantive or procedural, the temporal relationship between the matters, the significance of the issue to the immediate and long-term interests of the clients involved, and the clients' reasonable expectations in retaining the lawyer.[9]

♦ CONFLICTS BETWEEN PARTIES NOT IN LITIGATION

It may be more difficult to decide whether there is a conflict of interest in situations that do not involve litigation. A variety of contexts for possible conflict present themselves when litigation is not involved.

For example, a lawyer may be asked to represent a buyer and seller in a real estate transaction, multiple family members involved in estate planning, or multiple parties involved on the same side of a negotiation. The comment to ABA Model Rule 1.7 notes that a lawyer would be permitted to represent more than one party in negotiation if the parties are on the same side of that negotiation and their interests are aligned, even if there may be minor differences in their positions.[10]

In trying to determine whether representation might adversely affect a client when litigation is not involved, the relevant factors include the duration and intimacy of the lawyer's relationship with the client, the duties that the lawyer will perform, the likelihood that an actual conflict will arise, and the likely prejudice that will result to the client if a conflict develops.

♦ CURRENT VERSUS FORMER CLIENTS

The conflict of interest rules that apply to current representations are substantially more restrictive than those that apply to prior representations.

Without express consent, a law firm may not take a position adverse to a current client in any matter, even if the new matter is completely unrelated to services the law firm is performing for the client.[11] In contrast, a law firm may represent an interest adverse to that of a former client in any matter that is not the same matter or substantially related to the matter on which the law firm advised the client.[12]

♦ LAWYER'S OWN INTERESTS

With respect to a lawyer's own interests, the comment to ABA Model Rule 1.7 notes that it may be difficult or impossible for a lawyer to give objective advice when the integrity of the lawyer's own conduct is in question. For example, a court disqualified a lawyer who sat on the board of directors of a cable franchise affiliated with a defendant telecommunications company from representing the plaintiff class in an employment discrimination suit that alleged misdeeds by the company's affiliates. The court reasoned that the lawyer was essentially suing himself and may have been able to use the information gleaned from his director position to steer the litigation in a way that would limit his potential involvement as a defendant or witness.[13]

Conflicts with the lawyer's own interests also may arise out of direct business transactions with a client. ABA Model Rule 1.8(a) disallows such transactions unless they are objectively fair to the client, the client is given a clear written explanation of the terms, the client has an opportunity to consult independent counsel concerning the transaction, and the client consents in writing. Because of the perceived advantage that a lawyer has when doing business with a client and the duty of loyalty a lawyer owes to a client, lawyers are held to a very high standard of conduct by courts considering the fairness of a particular transaction and the lawyer's adherence to the requirements of the rule.

Paralegals also may have personal interests that create a conflict. The comment to Guideline 7 of the ABA *Model Guidelines for the Utilization of Paralegal Services* notes that lawyers "must ensure that paralegals are instructed to disclose an interest that could create an apparent or actual conflict of interest." This is an ongoing obligation, as conflicts can arise at any time after hire.

▸ INTEREST IN THE LITIGATION

The ABA Model Rules also generally prohibit lawyers from acquiring an interest in a client's cause of action or the subject matter of litigation.[14] However, there are important exceptions to the rule.

First, a lawyer may work on a contingent-fee basis under certain circumstances. A contingent fee is by definition based on the outcome of the matter. The primary basis for permitting contingent fees is that such an arrangement is often the only practical way that a party can obtain and afford the services of a competent lawyer and pursue a complicated or costly case.

Several requirements and restrictions regarding the establishment of a contingent fee arrangement are found in ABA Model Rule 1.5. Generally, the details of the agreement must be in writing,[15] and such an agreement may not be used in a domestic relations or criminal case.[16]

Furthermore, ABA Model Rule 1.8(e) allows a lawyer to advance court costs and litigation expenses, even on a contingent basis, and to assume responsibility for court costs and expenses of an indigent client. However, a lawyer is not permitted to advance living expenses for a client. As noted in an ABA ethics opinion,[17] allowing lawyers to advance living expenses would increase lawyers' stakes in the outcome of cases, which might in turn lead lawyers to consider their own recovery rather than that of the clients. For example, a lawyer might be tempted to urge a client to accept a settlement to ensure the lawyer's recovery of costs, rather than to proceed to trial and thereby risk the possibility that there may be no recovery at all.

Second, a lawyer is permitted to acquire certain liens to secure payment of legal fees and expenses,[18] although the assertion of a lien is subject to the ethics rules that require a lawyer, upon termination of representation, to take reasonable steps to protect a client's interests. The nature, extent, and application of such a lien is a question of state law.

◆ PERSONAL RELATIONSHIPS

A lawyer's personal—especially family—relationships may also create a conflict of interest. The commentary to ABA Model Rule 1.7 provides that a lawyer closely related to another lawyer—such as a parent, child, sibling, or spouse—ordinarily may not represent a client in a matter where the related lawyer is representing another party, unless each client gives informed consent. The focus of this commentary is that when lawyers representing different clients in the same matter or in substantially related matters are closely related by blood or marriage, there may be a significant risk that client confidences will be revealed and that the lawyer's family relationship will interfere with both loyalty and independent professional judgment. This prohibition is personal and is not usually imputed to the entire firm.

Paralegals also must take care when they are related to paralegals or lawyers on the opposing side of a case. There exists the same risk that is present with two opposing, related lawyers. As soon as a potential conflict surfaces, paralegals must notify their supervising lawyer.[19] Canon 3 of the National Association for Legal Assistants (NALA) Code of Ethics and Professional Responsibility requires that a paralegal avoid conduct that would cause the lawyer to be unethical or even appear to be unethical.

▶ SEXUAL RELATIONS WITH CLIENTS

Model Rule 1.8(j) provides that a "lawyer shall not have sexual relations with a client unless a consensual sexual relationship existed between them when the client-lawyer relationship commenced." The ban on such relationships recognizes the fiduciary nature of the client-lawyer relationship and the possibility that such a relationship may unfairly exploit the lawyer's position of trust and impair the lawyer's ability to exercise independent professional judgment. In addition, such a relationship, which blurs the line between professional and personal relationships, may erode the protection given to client confidences by the attorney-client privilege and impair the client's ability to give informed consent. Therefore, the rule prohibits lawyers from having sexual relations with a client, unless the relationship existed prior to the representation, regardless of whether the relationship is consensual and regardless of the absence of prejudice to the client.[20] While no such restriction applies to paralegals, NALA Canon 8 states that a "paralegal must disclose to his or her employer or prospective employer any pre-existing client or personal relationship that may conflict with the interests of the employer or prospective employer and/or their clients." This is another example of the importance of communication between the paralegal and the lawyer.

▶ GIFTS FROM CLIENTS

The ABA Model Rules explicitly prohibit lawyers from drafting a document on behalf of a client unrelated to the lawyer that gives the lawyer or the lawyer's close relative a substantial gift.[21] The primary concern is that the lawyer drafting the document is in a position to exert undue influence on the client. A lawyer who stands to gain from a document must insist that an independent lawyer draft it.[22]

Even though the rules do not prohibit direct gifts from clients, the comment to ABA Model Rule 1.8 states, in its discussion of business transactions, that a lawyer may accept a gift from a client only if the "transaction meets general standards of fairness." Reasonable gifts given as tokens of appreciation or holiday gifts may be accepted by a lawyer or a paralegal.

♦ LAWYERS AND PARALEGALS SWITCHING FIRMS

When firms and corporations hire individuals who have been employed by other firms, the information those individuals may have acquired at their previous place of employment is attributed or imputed to the other lawyers in the new firm as if they had acquired the information themselves. Thus, disqualification of a law firm based upon a firm member having information relating to and gained through the representation of an opposing party during previous employment is called imputed disqualification.

It is presumed that, because of the former firm's representation, the lawyer had access to confidential information about the case.[23] The risk of a conflict of interest grows with the number and size of previous employers.

Similar considerations are present when a paralegal changes firms. In order to protect the information related to the representation of a client at the paralegal's former firm, lawyers from both the new and old firms must take steps to prevent the paralegal's disclosure of that information.[24]

States differ on whether automatic disqualification of the paralegal's new law firm should result. In Florida, for example, a lawyer must admonish an employee who has accepted a job with an opposing firm not to disclose client information, and the new firm must not request or permit revelation of information.[25] Even so, the firm may be disqualified based upon an analysis similar to the one used when lawyers switch firms.[26] In Kansas, a law firm that has hired a nonlawyer from another firm that is its adversary in a pending case may continue to represent the adverse client as long as the client of the former firm consents and a screening device is used, or it can be proven that the employee did not acquire confidential information at the former firm.[27]

Most states do not automatically disqualify a firm based on a paralegal's previous employment by opposing counsel but instead engage in a balancing test to determine the risk of disclosure. Courts weigh whether the paralegal had access to information related to the representation at the prior firm and, if so,

- whether the paralegal actually acquired the information;
- whether the paralegal will be working on the same case at the new firm;
- whether protective screening measures have been implemented by the new firm to prevent the paralegal from revealing any such information;
- whether the former firm admonished the paralegal to reveal no information; and
- whether the paralegal has actually revealed any information related to the representation.[28]

Other states adopt the position that the exposure to information related to a representation creates the rebuttable presumption that the information was shared, and if screening measures are not sufficient, disqualification is the only way to protect the client information.[29]

SCREENING MEASURES

In refusing to strictly apply the rules for disqualifying a law firm based on a conflict of interest, courts have been guided by two considerations: a client's right to choose counsel[30] and the effect a strict rule would have on the ability of lawyers to change jobs.[31] As a result, some jurisdictions allow law firms to avoid imputed disqualification in certain circumstances by screening the involved lawyer from the rest of the firm, meaning that the lawyer does not discuss or have any contact with other members of the firm in regard to the matters that might otherwise cause the conflict and resulting disqualification of the firm.[32] In 2009, the ABA amended Model Rule 1.10 to permit the screening of lawyers under certain circumstances.

Screening is not just a matter of someone promising not to reveal information related to the representation of a client or of the law firm admonishing someone not to work on a matter.[33] Rather, it is a formal procedure established within the firm so that there is no real threat of disclosure of the information.[34] Thus, it should not merely be oral instructions[35] and may extend to the formation and management of a firm's data-keeping functions.

It has been suggested that passwords to electronic files should be withheld from screened employees and that periodic reminders of the screen be sent to all staff.[36] Model Rule 1.10 contains a provision regarding certifications of compliance with the rule and the screening procedures to be sent to the former client.

Effective creation of such an "ethical wall" limits the disqualification to the lawyer or paralegal who has the information. Other lawyers in the firm may represent the client free of any misuse of the information. Two factors to be considered in determining whether an ethical wall is likely to be successful are the size of the firm and the extent of its departmentalization. Other factors are whether the screened lawyer is able to gain access to the case files, shares in the profits or fees derived from the matter, is able to discuss the lawsuit with any of the members of the firm or office personnel, and is given the opportunity to review any of the case documents.

Paralegals are affected in three ways by this rule. First, it is important that each employee be made aware of any screening mechanisms that have been established at the firm so that the employee does not inadvertently communicate with a screened lawyer or other paralegal about matters that are not to be discussed.

Second, because paralegals also may be privy to protected information, some of the same concerns that apply to lawyers who change firms apply to them. Thus, there is the potential for a lawyer or law firm to be disqualified on the basis of a conflict created by the paralegal.[37] The newly hired employee may be asked to complete a questionnaire that will be used to check for potential conflicts. Whether or not the firm uses such a questionnaire, paralegals, as agents of the firm, must be forthcoming to their employers about their involvement in matters at a previous place of employment, because the law firm has a duty to advise its clients about potential conflicts, and the firm may need to take steps to avoid disqualification.

Paralegals can be screened just as lawyers are, although, depending upon the paralegal's position within the firm, there may be less chance of disqualification.[38] However, in most jurisdictions that allow screening, the screen must be in place before there is an opportunity for disclosure of protected information in order to avoid disqualification.[39] This highlights the importance of the paralegal advising a new employer about all the matters that the paralegal worked on at prior firms.

And the screen must be effective. A law firm that sets up a screen in regard to a newly hired paralegal may still be disqualified from a case when the paralegal winds up working on a case that he or she had previously worked on for the opposing law firm.[40] No matter how minimal the contact with the screened matter, disqualification could result. If given an assignment that appears to present a conflict, the paralegal should advise the supervising lawyer of the potential problem before the damage is done.

Third, a paralegal who works closely with a lawyer who is being screened may have access to protected information and therefore also need to be screened.

In establishing an ethical wall, a law firm may require that paralegals sign an affidavit stating that

- they will have no contact with certain files (the firm must take steps to keep the files, including electronic ones,[41] in a secure place);
- they will not discuss the files with anyone in the firm; and
- they will not disclose any information acquired at the previous firm.

The paralegal is subject to the same restrictions as a lawyer who is being screened.

It may not always be clear whether information is protected. It is not just facts about a client or case but also legal analysis and case strategy developed by the previous firm that may be protected. It is wise to err on the side of caution if one is unsure whether information is protected.

It also may not always be clear whether any two matters have the "substantial relationship" referred to in Model Rule 1.9. If a paralegal has any doubt whether information is protected, he or she should consult with the supervising lawyer, because the ramifications of revealing protected information extend not only to potential professional liability and disciplinary sanctions against the lawyer but also to economic loss and loss of clients for the firm.

◆ CONFLICT OF INTEREST CHECKING SYSTEMS

Each time a prospective client or matter is brought to the firm, a conflict of interest check should be conducted. Otherwise, the lawyers and paralegals may start working on a matter before realizing there is a conflict. Each new staff member needs to check the list of clients to see if by working on a case for the lawyer a conflict could arise from information they obtained about the opposing party while working for another employer.

> **Checking for Possible Conflicts of Interest**
>
> ▼ A conflict of interest checking system should include relevant information about the following:
>
> ► current clients
>
> ► former clients
>
> ► prospective clients
>
> ► all other protected persons, such as spouses, partners, or shareholders or directors and officers of corporations
>
> ► additional parties brought into the matter that need to be added to the system
>
> ► information about the law firm staff assigned to the case

Whether a conflicts-checking system is computerized or manual, it should contain certain basic information. (See "Checking for Possible Conflicts of Interest" above for a list of entities and persons about whom a conflict of interest checking system typically contains information.[42]) The system should include a generic list of all matters handled by the firm and the clients for which these matters have been handled. It is extremely important that the list be kept current. The firm should publish a new matter sheet daily or weekly. The list should include all parties and known potential parties to matters and provide a summary of the case. In the case of corporate clients, notice should be taken not only of the client itself but also of any parent, subsidiary, or otherwise affiliated corporate entity.[43] All legal staff, lawyers, and paralegals should review the sheet, noting conflicts and notifying the responsible lawyer.

CHAPTER SUMMARY

☑ As soon as a potential conflict surfaces, a paralegal must notify his or her supervising lawyer.

☑ A personal relationship with a lawyer or paralegal on the opposing side of a case may present a conflict.

☑ Prior employment by an opposing law firm may present a conflict.

☑ It is important to be aware of and completely comply with any screening mechanisms in place at the law firm.

☑ It is important to be familiar with and comply with the law firm's conflict of interest checking system.

NOTES

1. *See* Hendry v. Pelland, 73 F.3d 397 (D.C. Cir. 1996) ("[A] basic fiduciary obligation of an attorney is the duty of 'undivided loyalty,' which is breached when an attorney represents clients with conflicting interests."); State *ex rel* S.G., 814 A.2d 612 (N.J. 2003) ("[A]ttorney-client relationship is grounded in the fundamental understanding that an attorney will give 'complete and undivided loyalty to the client. . . .'").

2. *See, e.g.*, ABA Comm. on Ethics & Prof'l Responsibility, Formal Op. 367 (1992) (generally, a lawyer may not represent a client if the representation will entail cross-examining another client as an adverse witness); *see also* Mass. Bar Ass'n, Ethics Comm., Op. 92-3 (1992) (law firm may not switch over to a long-term

client's side when it finds that its representation of a newer client has produced a conflict of interest).

3. See Model Rules of Prof'l Conduct R. 1.7, 1.8, 1.9 (2013).

4. See Memphis & Shelby Cnty. Bar Ass'n v. Sanderson, 378 S.W.2d 173 (Tenn. Ct. App. 1963); see also In re Hull, 767 A.2d 197 (Del. 2001) (direct conflict when lawyer representing husband and wife in bankruptcy proceeding filed motion to sever and transfer action on behalf of wife without husband's consent).

5. See I.B.M. v. Levin, 579 F.2d 271 (3d Cir. 1978).

6. ABA Comm. on Ethics & Prof'l Responsibility, Formal Op. 377 (1993).

7. ABA Standards for Criminal Justice 4-1.7 (2015) (lawyers should ordinarily decline joint representation in criminal cases except in unusual situations where prior investigation by the lawyer makes it clear that no conflict is likely to develop).

8. ABA Comm. on Ethics & Prof'l Responsibility, Formal Op. 377 (1993).

9. Model Rules of Prof'l Conduct R. 1.7 cmt. 24 (2013).

10. Id. cmt. 28.

11. Id.

12. Model Rules of Prof'l Conduct R. 1.9 cmt. 3 (2013).

13. Palumbu v. Tele-Communications, Inc., 157 F.R.D. 129 (D.D.C. 1994).

14. Model Rules of Prof'l Conduct R. 1.8(i) (2013).

15. See Model Rules of Prof'l Conduct R. 1.5(c) (2013).

16. See Model Rules of Prof'l Conduct R. 1.5(d).

17. ABA Formal Ethics Opinion 288 (1954).

18. See, e.g., Giles v. Russell, 567 P.2d 845 (Kan. 1977) (lien on property as additional security for compensation and reimbursement of expenses under employment agreement conforms to requirements).

19. See Nat'l Fed'n of Paralegal Ass'ns Model Code of Ethics & Prof'l Responsibility EC-1.6(a)–(g).

20. Model Rules of Prof'l Conduct R. 1.18(i) cmt. 17 (2013); see, e.g., In re Rinella, 677 N.E.2d 909 (Ill. 1997) (lawyer who engaged in sexual relations with three clients while representing them in matrimonial matters overreached and took advantage of his position).

21. Model Rules of Prof'l Conduct R. 1.8(c).

22. In re Boulger, 637 N.W.2d 710 (N.D. 2001) (lawyer engaged in misconduct by drafting will codicil with provisions giving lawyer substantial contingent testamentary gift even though contingencies to trigger testamentary gift were so unlikely to happen that it was improbable lawyer would receive anything under will); Comm. on Legal Ethics v. Veneri, 411 S.E.2d 865 (W. Va. 1991) (lawyer's multiple roles as lawyer for, executor of, and beneficiary of his mother's estate presented conflict of interest; note: the family context did not excuse this conflict).

23. Laws. Man. on Prof. Conduct (ABA/BNA) 51:2009 (Feb. 17, 2010). See also Chapter 6 regarding what may be revealed by a lawyer switching firms in order to detect conflicts of interest.

24. See Model Rules of Prof'l Conduct R. 1.10 cmt. 4 (2013) (providing that nonlawyer employees who obtain disqualifying information are disqualified

personally, but the conflict is not imputed so long as they are screened from participation in the matter).

25. Prof'l Ethics Comm. of the Fla. Bar, Op. 86-5 (1986).

26. See Koulisis v. Rivers, 730 So. 2d 289 (Fla. Dist. Ct. App. 1999). There is a difference of opinion among the Florida district courts as to the presumptions that should be used regarding a paralegal's knowledge of confidential information. See Lansing v. Lansing, 784 So. 2d 1254 (Fla. Dist. Ct. App. 2001), and First Miami Sec., Inc. v. Sylvia, 780 So. 2d 250 (Fla. Dist. Ct. App. 2001), for discussions of the different standards.

27. Zimmerman v. Mahaska Bottling Co., 19 P.3d 784 (Kan. 2001); Kan. Bar Ass'n Prof'l Ethics Advisory Comm., Op. 2002-01 (2002); see also Leibowitz v. Eighth Judicial Dist. Court of Nev., 78 P.3d 515 (Nev. 2003) (detailing minimum requirements for effective screening and instructing firms implementing screens to notify the affected client or the client's counsel); Tenn. Supreme Court Bd. of Prof'l Responsibility, Formal Op., 2003-F-147 (2003) (advising that imputed disqualification and screening rules apply to nonlawyers in firm).

28. ABA Comm. on Ethics & Prof'l Responsibility, Informal Op. 88-1526 (1988); see Leibowitz, 78 P.3d 515 (no disqualification); In re Complex Asbestos Litig., 283 Cal. Rptr. 732 (Ct. App. 1991) (disqualification); Grant v. 13th Court of Appeals, 888 S.W.2d 466 (Tex. 1994) (disqualification); Esquire Care, Inc. v. Maguire, 532 So. 2d 740 (Fla. Dist. Ct. App. 1988) (no disqualification).

29. In re Am. Home Prods. Corp., 985 S.W.2d 68 (Tex. 1998) (law firm unable to rebut presumption that confidential information was disclosed by a paralegal who switched sides); Williams v. Trans World Airlines, Inc., 588 F. Supp. 1037 (W.D. Mo. 1984) (threat of taint sufficient to disqualify plaintiff's firm when defendant firm's legal assistant switches employment); Parker v. Volkswagenwerk Aktiengesellschaft, 781 P.2d 1099 (Kan. 1989) (unilateral screening insufficient; nonlawyer must also show he did not obtain confidential information in previous employment); Glover Bottled Gas Corp. v. Circle M. Beverage Barn, Inc., 514 N.Y.S.2d 440 (Sup. Ct. 1987) (paralegal who worked on litigation for plaintiff and interviewed plaintiff's manager is tainted and disqualifies defendant's firm from representation).

30. See, e.g., Ness, Motley, Loadholt, Richardson & Poole P.A. v. Aetna Cas. & Sur. Co., No. A3-88-157 (D. Kan. Aug. 8, 1990), reported in Laws. Man. on Prof. Conduct (ABA/BNA), 6 Current Rep. 324 (Oct. 10, 1990); Donohoe v. Consol. Operating & Prod. Corp., 691 F. Supp. 109 (N.D. Ill. 1988); Lemaire v. TEXACO, INC., 496 F. SUPP. 1308 (E.D. TEX. 1980).

31. See Manning v. Waring, Cox, James, Sklar & Allen, 849 F.2d 222 (6th Cir. 1988).

32. See, e.g., Schiessle v. Stephens, 717 F.2d 417 (7th Cir. 1983); Gerald v. Turnock Plumbing, Heating & Cooling, LLC, 768 N.E.2d 498 (Ind. App. 2002); Kala v. Aluminum Smelting & Ref. Co., 688 N.E.2d 258 (Ohio 1998).

33. In re Columbia Valley Healthcare Sys., L.P., 320 S.W.3d 819 (Tex. 2010).

34. See, e.g., Grant v. 13th Court of Appeals, 888 S.W.2d 466 (Tex. 1994) (Texas Supreme Court disqualified a firm based upon a conflict caused by the hiring

of a legal secretary despite unrebutted testimony that no confidences had been revealed; court noted that appropriate screening mechanisms had not been established).

35. In re Columbia Valley Healthcare Sys., 320 S.W.3d 819.

36. L.A. Cnty. Bar Ass'n Prof'l Responsibility & Ethics Comm. Op. No. 524 (May 16, 2011).

37. See, e.g., Kapco Mfg. Co. v. C & O Enters., 637 F. Supp. 1231 (N.D. Ill. 1985); Herron v. Jones, 637 S.W.2d 569 (Ark. 1982).

38. See Hodge v. Urfa-Sexton, LP, 758 S.E.2d 314 (Ga. 2014); Esquire Care, Inc. v. Maguire, 532 So. 2d 740 (Fla. Dist. Ct. App. 1988); Phx. Founders, Inc. v. Marshall, 887 S.W.2d 831 (Tex. 1994); ABA Comm. on Ethics & Prof'l Responsibility, Informal Op. 1526 (1988).

39. See, e.g., E Z Painter Corp. v. Padco, Inc., 746 F.2d 1459 (Fed. Cir. 1984); Haagen-Dazs Co. v. Perche No! Gelato, Inc., 639 F. Supp. 282 (N.D. Cal. 1986); USFL v. NFL, 605 F. Supp. 1448 (S.D.N.Y. 1985). The rule in Washington is different, permitting implementation of a screen after employment, as long as there is convincing evidence that there was no disclosure before the screening and the screen, once implemented, is effective. See Daines v. Alcatel, S.A., 194 F.R.D. 678 (E.D. Wash. 2000).

40. In re Guar. Ins. Servs., Inc., 310 S.W.3d 630 (Tex. App.–Austin 2010).

41. See, e.g., Rubin v. Enns, 23 S.W.3d 382 (Tex. App.–Amarillo 2000) (firm removed all references to the underlying cases from the firm's computer system).

42. For more on conflicts of interest checking systems, see ABA Legal Technology Resource Center, *FYI: Conflict Checking*, ABA, http://www.americanbar.org/groups/departments_offices/legal_technology_resources/resources/charts_fyis/coninterestfyi.html; Todd C. Scott, *Conflict-Checking Systems: Three Great (and Cheap) Ways to Effectively Manage Conflict Checking*, 2 GP SOLO LAW TRENDS & NEWS 2 (2006), available at http://www.americanbar.org/newsletter/publications/law_trends_news_practice_area_e_newsletter_home/conflictchecking.html.

43. See ABA Comm. on Ethics & Prof'l Responsibility, Formal Op. 390 (1995), for a discussion of conflicts of interest in the corporate family context.

Chapter EIGHT

Communications

COMMUNICATIONS WITH CLIENTS

Communications play an important role in any client-lawyer relationship. As stated in ABA Model Rule 1.4, lawyers have an obligation to keep clients reasonably informed about their representation, to reasonably consult with clients about the means used to attain their objectives, and to promptly comply with reasonable client requests for information.

Many of the complaints that lawyer disciplinary agencies receive about lawyers from clients relate to a perceived lack of communication on behalf of the lawyers.[1] In order to help avoid these kinds of complaints, it is important that paralegals keep their supervising lawyers informed about communications received from clients and relay any information directed to clients from the lawyers in an accurate and timely fashion.

Communications with Others outside the Client-Lawyer Relationship

In addition to understanding what is expected regarding communications with clients and with supervising lawyers, paralegals must be aware of the ethical restrictions regarding communications with others who have some relationship to the matter being handled.

Communications with Judges

Lawyers generally are prohibited from communicating during a proceeding with judges and others serving in an official capacity in the proceeding without notifying opposing parties and giving them the opportunity to be present. This prohibition on ex parte communications applies equally to the paralegal. The paralegal who is assisting with a matter at the courthouse must be careful not to initiate or respond to any such communications. Lawyers have been disciplined for ex parte communications with judges by nonlawyers associated on a matter with the lawyer.[2]

There are, however, limited exceptions to this prohibition, such as when ex parte communication is authorized by law or court order. Under these exceptions, ex parte communications with judges may be permitted for routine administrative matters, such as scheduling hearings.[3]

Unauthorized Communications with Jurors and Prospective Jurors

Lawyers' communications with jurors and prospective jurors are subject to restrictions.[4] Different restrictions apply depending upon whether or not the proceeding is still pending.

Communication during Pending Proceedings

Model Rule 3.5(b) states that "[a] lawyer shall not communicate ex parte with [a juror or prospective juror] during the proceeding unless authorized to do so by law or court order."

As to what qualifies as communication, the ABA has issued an opinion that discusses this in the context of lawyers reviewing jurors' Internet presence. The opinion states:

> A lawyer may not, either personally or through another, send an access request to a juror's electronic social media. An access request is a communication to a juror asking the juror for information that the juror has not made public and that would be the type of ex parte communication prohibited by Model Rule 3.5(b). The fact that a juror or a potential juror may become aware that a lawyer is reviewing his Internet presence when a network setting notifies the juror of such does not constitute a communication from the lawyer in violation of Rule 3.5(b).[5]

This last conclusion is not universal. There is a view that the existence of such a notification may constitute a communication between the lawyer and juror or prospective juror.[6]

If the lawyer or paralegal already is a member of the juror or potential juror's social network, the question then is whether there needs to be disclosure to the juror or prospective juror about this relationship. On the surface, it seems unnecessary to have to disclose to someone that you are a "friend," but, in today's world, where people create social networks that include hundreds or thousands of connections, it is not that hard to imagine someone not recalling that another person, whom they barely know, is part of their network.

If a lawyer asks a paralegal to do Internet investigation about a juror or prospective juror, the paralegal must be careful to follow the rules in their jurisdiction regarding such communication.

Communication after Discharge of the Jury

After the jury is discharged, Model Rule 3.5(c) permits a lawyer to communicate with jurors and prospective jurors unless doing so is prohibited by law or court order; the juror has made known a desire not to communicate; or the communication involves misrepresentation, coercion, duress, or harassment.

Thus, in applying these principles, one state ethics opinion has offered that "[a] lawyer . . . may assign a paralegal from the firm to telephone jurors for post-trial interviews provided that the interviews are conducted without intimidating or pressuring the jurors."[7]

Communication with Person Represented by Counsel

To help preserve the client-lawyer relationship, lawyers generally are prohibited from communicating about a matter in which they are involved with anyone who is represented by another lawyer in that matter unless that other lawyer consents to the communication.[8] A lawyer may not circumvent this rule by communicating through a third person.[9] Thus, a paralegal must not act as go-between in an effort by a lawyer at the paralegal's law firm to contact the person being represented by another lawyer. Failure to abide by this rule can have various consequences, including the assessment of fees and costs against the law firm and the prohibition of the use of the information gathered by the paralegal as a result of the communication.[10] An exception to the rule may exist because of other law or a court order, but a paralegal should not assume that one exists unless provided with specific evidence. Accordingly, if asked to do some investigation related to a matter, the paralegal must keep in mind the restrictions of Model Rule 4.2.

If the opposing party is one that has an obligation to provide information separate and apart from the matter in controversy, such as a government agency, then the communication is permissible.

A lawyer whose firm represents a private party in a matter against a state agency that is represented by the attorney general may direct the firm's paralegal to contact an employee of the agency and request, under the state's Freedom of Information Act, certain records relevant to the proceeding.[11]

"In the committee's view, the status of litigant or litigant's counsel does not disenfranchise one from obtaining information otherwise available to the public."[12]

Who Is a Represented Person?

An obvious question is who, other than a party, would be represented in a matter. Generally, this can be anyone who is a witness or potential witness. If that person happens to be employed by an organization that is represented in the matter, the person may be considered to be represented by the organization's lawyers. But this will depend on a number of factors related to that person's responsibilities and authority.[13] The lawyer will have to analyze those factors, but it is good for the paralegal to be aware of the general principle that communications with certain employees of the opposing party are prohibited.

Communication through Social Media

Similar considerations in regard to Model Rule 3.5 apply to the application of Model Rule 4.2. Thus, just as one may view the public pages of a juror or prospective juror's social network, it is not considered a communication with a represented party for a lawyer or paralegal involved in a matter to view the public pages of the social network of a person known to be represented by another lawyer in the matter.[14]

On the other hand, a request by a lawyer or paralegal to view the private portion of a represented person's social network would be a violation of the rule.[15] Because deception is not a necessary element of a violation of this rule, even if the lawyer or paralegal clearly states his or her name and the purpose of the request, the conduct violates the rule against communication with a represented party.

Communication with Unrepresented Person

If a person is not represented by counsel, the rules are different. Communication is permitted. Lawyers have a responsibility when representing a client, however, not to mislead people who are not represented by counsel into believing that the lawyer is disinterested.[16]

The lawyer's duty includes not giving legal advice to someone other than the client if there is a possibility of a conflict between that person's interests and those of the client. One area where a paralegal may become involved is in the submission of documents on behalf of the lawyer to the unrepresented person. While the comments to the rule make it clear that a lawyer may prepare documents for the unrepresented person's signature, the lawyer must make it clear that the lawyer is representing the adverse party and not that other person. The paralegal must be careful not to say or do anything that reasonably could be interpreted otherwise by the other person.

A lawyer must clearly state his or her identity and purpose to the unrepresented person. Any deception or omission may be seen as implying disinterest. This includes the situation in which a request is made to access someone's social networking site.[17]

◆ TRUTHFULNESS IN STATEMENTS TO OTHERS

A paralegal should be wary of an instruction to use deception when communicating with others under any circumstances. ABA Model Rule 8.4 states that it is misconduct "for a lawyer to engage in conduct involving dishonesty, fraud, deceit or misrepresentation." A lawyer's use of a paralegal in contravention of this rule constitutes a violation.[18]

Lawyers also have an obligation to be truthful to others in the course of representing clients by not making false statements of material fact and disclosing material facts when necessary to avoid assisting a criminal or fraudulent act.[19] This duty can surface in many different situations. One common, yet complicated, situation is that involving negotiations, where some statements are generally not to be taken as material facts.[20] It would be unfair to ask a paralegal to be responsible for determining whether statements are to be taken as material facts or to determine the truth of statements that the paralegal may be communicating at the direction of a lawyer, but the paralegal should be careful to communicate any information from the lawyer accurately and to refrain from adding anything to a communication that might affect its truthfulness.

◆ PUBLIC COMMUNICATIONS

Those who watch lawyer television shows might believe that every case that lawyers handle is the subject of great media interest and that lawyers often speak to the press about their cases. Though that is not an accurate depiction, a law firm may become involved in a high-profile case that draws media attention. And, although constitutional protections regarding the freedom of speech do apply, some restrictions on what lawyers may say publicly about a matter in which they are participating are permissible.[21] This is a separate and additional restriction from that regarding confidentiality, as discussed in Chapter 6. It has to do with the likelihood of materially prejudicing an adjudicative proceeding and involves a number of considerations.[22] Thus, as with issues regarding confidentiality, the safest course of action is for a paralegal to avoid making any public statements about a matter in which the law firm is involved.

Communications

CHAPTER SUMMARY

- ☑ Paralegals must keep their supervising lawyers informed about communications received from clients and relay any information directed to clients from the lawyers in an accurate and timely fashion.

- ☑ Paralegals must be careful not to get involved in prohibited ex parte communications with judges.

- ☑ A paralegal may not send an access request to the electronic social media of a juror or prospective juror in a proceeding involving a client of the paralegal's firm.

- ☑ After trial, a paralegal may not communicate with one of the jurors if prohibited by law or court order; the juror has made known a desire not to communicate; or the communication involves misrepresentation, coercion, duress, or harassment.

- ☑ A paralegal may not communicate about the subject of a representation with a person known to be represented by a lawyer in the matter, unless that lawyer consents or there is authority to do so by law or a court order.

- ☑ An employee of an organization may be considered to be represented by the counsel representing the organization for purposes of the rule on communication depending on the responsibilities and authority of the employee.

- ☑ A paralegal may communicate with an unrepresented person but generally may not be deceptive, including not stating or implying that the paralegal's law firm is disinterested in the matter being discussed.

- ☑ A paralegal should be wary of an instruction to use deception when communicating with others under any circumstances.

- ☑ A paralegal should avoid making any public statements about a matter in which the law firm is involved.

▶ NOTES

1. *See* THE ATTORNEY REGISTRATION AND DISCIPLINARY COMMISSION OF THE SUPREME COURT OF ILLINOIS 2012 ANNUAL REPORT, *available at* https://www.iardc.

org/AnnualReport2012.pdf ("More than half of all grievances filed involved issues of poor attorney-client relations, typically neglect of a client matter (38% of all grievances) or failure to communicate with a client (20% of all grievances)."); Scott Morrill, *Complaints About Oregon Lawyers: 2011 Trends from the OSB's Client Assistance Office*, OR. ST. B. BULL. (Apr. 2012), *available at* http://www.osbar.org/publications/bulletin/12apr/barcounsel.html ("The number one complaint for 2011 was lack of communication. About 10 percent of all complaints in 2011 . . . were that a lawyer was not adequately communicating or responding to requests for information about the client's legal matter.").

2. *See, e.g.*, In re Beck, 109 So. 3d 897 (La. 2013) (lawyer suspended after admitting that he did not discourage the ex parte communication between accountant associated with the lawyer and judge presiding over trial litigated by the lawyer).

3. *See, e.g.*, MODEL CODE OF JUDICIAL CONDUCT R. 2.9(A)(1) (2007) (authorizing judges to engage in ex parte communication in certain circumstances "for scheduling, administrative, or emergency purposes").

4. MODEL RULES OF PROF'L CONDUCT R. 3.5 (2013).

5. ABA Comm. on Ethics & Prof'l Responsibility, Formal Op. 466 (2014).

6. *See, e.g.*, N.Y. Cnty. Lawyers Ass'n, Formal Op. 743 (2011).

7. Pa. Op. 91-52 (Apr. 3, 1991).

8. MODEL RULES OF PROF'L CONDUCT R. 4.2 (2013).

9. ABA Formal Ethics Op. 95-396 (1995).

10. Penda Corp. v. STK, LLC, 2004 WL 1628907 (E.D. Pa. 2004).

11. Va. Op. 1504 (Dec. 14, 1992).

12. *Id.*

13. *See* MODEL RULES OF PROF'L CONDUCT R. 4.2 cmt. 7 (2013).

14. Or. State Bar Ass'n, Formal Op. 2013-189.

15. San Diego Cnty. Bar Legal Ethics Op. 2011-2 (concluding that a lawyer is prohibited from making an ex parte friend request of a represented party to view the nonpublic portions of a social networking website).

16. MODEL RULES OF PROF'L CONDUCT R. 4.3 (2013).

17. *See* Pa. Formal Op. 2014-300 ("[A] lawyer may not use deception to gain access to an unrepresented person's social networking site. A lawyer may ethically request access to the site, however, by using the lawyer's real name and by stating the lawyer's purpose for the request. Omitting the purpose would imply that the lawyer is disinterested, contrary to Rule 4.3(a).").

18. Peter Vieth, *Prosecutor Accepts Reprimand from Bar*, VA. LAWS. WKLY., Mar. 20, 2013 (prosecutor acknowledged that he engaged in misrepresentation when he sent his paralegal to ask questions at an adversary's office under the pretense of taking a college survey).

19. MODEL RULES OF PROF'L CONDUCT R. 4.1 (2013).

20. *Id.* cmt. 2.

21. *See* Gentile v. State Bar, 501 U.S. 1030 (1991).

22. MODEL RULES OF PROF'L CONDUCT R. 3.6 (2013).

Chapter NINE

Information about Legal Services

▶ As part of the legal team, a paralegal must understand and abide by the lawyer advertising rules to avoid ethical problems. With a proper understanding of these rules, a paralegal can play an important role in marketing the law firm's services and ensuring that the firm's marketing activities are conducted in an ethical manner.

Advertising legal services is a controversial issue within the legal profession that has led to substantial regulatory activity and numerous court challenges. Many lawyers strongly believe that advertising undermines the dignity of the legal profession. Others argue that it not only allows law firms to operate as businesses but also provides an important consumer benefit.

Ethics rules in this area frequently differ from one state to another, though all states prohibit advertising and marketing that is false or misleading. The rules apply to everything from the names of law firms and the use of names and titles on law firm letterhead and business cards to the solicitation of clients. New issues, such as marketing in cyberspace, continue to arise.

Lawyer advertising was banned for most of the 20th century. In 1977, the U.S. Supreme Court ruled, in *Bates v. State Bar of Arizona*,[1] that states could not ban lawyers from exercising their First Amendment right of commercial free speech by truthful advertising of their services to the public.

Before the *Bates* case, lawyers in most states could have only simple listings in telephone directories, dignified business cards and announcements, and signs outside their office. The ethics provisions encouraged lawyers to develop clients by demonstrating good service and by the "establishment of a well-merited reputation for professional capacity and fidelity to trust"[2] rather than by advertising. Today, however, legal services are marketed in a wide variety of ways, ranging from direct mail to newspaper advertisements to Internet ads to polished video productions detailing a firm's capabilities.

Even though many lawyers may be philosophically opposed to lawyer advertising, an increasing number work in firms that advertise and market their services. It is therefore important for those who work in law firms to know about the regulations that govern these areas.

▶ Nature and Scope of Lawyer Advertising Regulations

The regulations that govern what lawyers are permitted to do in their advertising, solicitation, and marketing endeavors are part of the rules of legal ethics that apply to all lawyers. Following are three issues that are fundamental to an understanding of these regulations.

Regulations Governing Lawyer Advertising Are Broad

The states' rules that regulate lawyer communications about services are often referred to in the legal profession as the "advertising rules." In fact, however, these rules are broad in scope and govern all communications by the law firm, as well as its employees and agents, that involve a commercial transaction. In other words, all law firm marketing activities are subject to the ethics rules. This could include newsletters, firm brochures, and even holiday greeting cards that are sent out by a firm. It could include sponsoring a booth at a convention, writing an article for a magazine, or giving a speech to a community organization. Lawyers and paralegals who are working with issues of lawyer advertising and law firm marketing must keep in mind that the ethics rules go beyond "lawyer advertising" and govern a wide range of activities.

Regulations Governing Lawyer Advertising Vary State by State

Like the other ethics rules governing the conduct of lawyers, those that address advertising, solicitation, and marketing are adopted on a state-by-state basis. As a result, advertising activities that may be ethical in one state may be unethical in another. In today's legal profession, where more and more firms have multijurisdictional practices, knowing the differences between the rules of each state where the firm's advertising or marketing takes place becomes increasingly important. The ABA Center for Professional Responsibility maintains an online document that keeps track of the differences between the state rules and the Model Rules.[3]

Regulations Governing Lawyer Advertising Change from Time to Time

Just as the regulations are different from one state to another, states may change their regulations from time to time. While this may be true of any of the ethics rules, it is particularly significant in this area where change has been frequent.

There are a variety of reasons for these changes. Several of the changes that have taken place over the past two decades have resulted from U.S. Supreme Court decisions.[4] Frequently, the Court has held that state regulations were too restrictive. These decisions have required the states to change their rules to permit greater freedom for lawyers to advertise. In other instances, states change their rules to respond to new marketing developments, such as the advent of new technologies like e-mail and the Internet.

◆ PROHIBITIONS OF COMMUNICATIONS THAT ARE FALSE OR MISLEADING

The most fundamental regulation governing lawyer advertising and legal services marketing is the prohibition against false or misleading communications. Although the specific state rules vary, each state has a provision of this nature. It may seem obvious that lawyers cannot advertise in ways that are not truthful or that are deceptive since states have consumer protection statutes that require this for many products and services. However, the legal profession has taken this standard to a higher level in several respects.

For example, ABA Model Rule 7.1 indicates that a communication is false or misleading if it "contains a material misrepresentation of fact or law, or omits a fact necessary to make the statement considered as a whole not materially misleading."

As an example of this standard, consider lawyers who provide legal services on a contingent fee basis, such as personal injury or workers' compensation representation, and who advertise that they charge no attorneys' fees if the case is not successfully settled or tried.[5] Most lawyers will charge clients for the costs of bringing the claim, whether or not they are successful. Since consumers of legal services may not distinguish between fees and costs, it could be misleading to omit information in an advertisement that clients are responsible for costs, when the lawyer advertises "no recovery, no fee."

Lawyers should also avoid creating unjustified expectations in their marketing efforts. Comment 3 to ABA Model Rule 7.1 states that an otherwise true statement may be misleading if presented in a way that would lead a reasonable person to form an unjustified expectation that the lawyer can obtain the same results for that person as the lawyer obtained in previous matters "without reference to the specific factual and legal circumstances of each client's case." The underlying assumption of the comment is that each legal matter is unique and that a lawyer's past performance is not an accurate measure of how the lawyer will be able to resolve a particular client's matter in the future. Therefore, a lawyer may not present information about past performance in a manner likely to lead a prospective client to believe that the same results can be achieved for him or her irrespective of the particular facts of the case.[6]

Unjustified expectations may be created in a number of ways.

First, a lawyer might advertise that his or her last case resulted in a settlement of $1 million, but it would be inappropriate to state that fact in such a way as to imply that the next case would have a similar result, since each legal matter is different. This would create an unjustified expectation.[7] Some policy makers are so concerned with the possibility of creating these expectations that, in some states, they have banned or otherwise regulated client endorsements and testimonials.[8]

Second, lawyers who are former judges frequently are referred to as "former Judge Doe" in their marketing materials. If a lawyer with a mediation service is referred to as a former judge, for example, that would be appropriate. However, if the lawyer is in private practice and the implication is that the lawyer can take advantage of his or her formal judicial position—for example, by obtaining favorable considerations from former judicial colleagues—that would inappropriately create an unjustified expectation. The same concern may apply to advertising references to other elected or appointed offices.

Third, firms should be careful not to use unsupportable absolute terms or to overstate their capacities. For example, firms should be wary of claiming that they are general practitioners who handle all areas of practice. Unlike advertising for products, where some degree of "puffing" is permissible, the legal profession strictly prohibits such exaggeration. According to comment 3 of ABA Model Rule 7.1, an unsubstantiated comparison of a lawyer's fees or services with those of others "may be misleading if presented with such specificity as would lead a reasonable person to conclude that the comparison can be substantiated." So lawyers generally cannot say that they are "the best," "the smartest," or "most efficient" unless they can factually substantiate the representation. In some cases interpreting the scope of this rule, lawyers' use of several subjective adjectives have been found to be unethical—even seemingly neutral terms such as "trustworthy" and "competent."[9]

However, there are numerous organizations that promote ratings of lawyers.[10] State bar ethics opinions considering the issue have determined that it is not false or misleading for a lawyer to state that he or she has been listed in a particular rating as long as it is true.[11]

If a paralegal is asked to input, proofread, or review marketing materials, he or she should take extra care to ensure that there is nothing false or misleading. Lawyers have been disciplined and court costs assessed based upon the failure to properly supervise a nonlawyer assistant who posted false, deceptive, and misleading information on the firm's website.[12]

◆ LIMITS ON FIRM NAMES AND USE OF FIRM LETTERHEAD

Law firm names, letterhead, and business cards are regulated by ABA Model Rule 7.5. The rule applies the "false and misleading" standard to firm names, letterhead, and other designations.

A trade name, such as the Springfield Legal Clinic, may be used, according to the Model Rules, so long as the name "does not imply a connection with a government agency or with a public or charitable legal services organization and is not otherwise in violation of Rule 7.1," which prohibits false or misleading representations.

A law firm with offices in more than one state can use the same name in each of the states but must be careful to clarify in which states individual lawyers are licensed to practice and not misrepresent the firm's capacity in any particular location.[13]

Under the ABA Model Rules and the opinions of states that have considered the issue, a law firm may continue to use the names of deceased partners in the firm name. However, the comments to the Model Rules indicate that it is inappropriate to continue to use in the firm name the name of someone who has otherwise left the firm. Similarly, the rules prohibit the use of the name of a lawyer who holds public office and is not "actively and regularly practicing with the firm."[14]

It is also misleading for a lawyer to imply a greater capacity than exists by operating under the name of the lawyer "and associates" if there are no associates.[15]

The Model Rules do not specifically address the propriety of using the names of paralegals and other law firm staff on letterhead or business cards. Some state ethics opinions have disapproved of including the names of nonlawyers on letterhead under any circumstances. Other states, however, go so far as to allow paralegals to include information about their certification, provided that the communication is not misleading.[16]

Therefore, at a minimum, it is essential that staff titles be included on letterhead and business cards in ways that are prominent and make the status of the staff clear and unambiguous. Any firm that plans to include paralegals on letterhead or issue them business cards should check the applicable state rules.[17]

The rules governing misleading representations must also be considered when a paralegal is the signatory of correspondence on firm letterhead. The appropriate course is to identify the staff position or title after the name of the signatory—for example, "James Jones, Paralegal." If a paralegal does not properly identify himself or herself, he or she may run the risk of being accused of the unauthorized practice of law.

♦ Limits on Solicitation of Clients

All jurisdictions have rules setting limits on the solicitation of clients. Some of the provisions contain outright prohibitions. ABA Model Rule 7.3(a) states:

- A lawyer shall not by in-person, live telephone or real-time electronic contact solicit professional employment when a significant motive for the lawyer's doing so is the lawyer's pecuniary gain, unless the person contacted: (1) is a lawyer; or (2) has a family, close personal, or prior professional relationship with the lawyer.

Nevertheless, certain types of solicitation of clients are generally permissible:

- written solicitations such as brochures, newsletters, and direct targeted mail, whether the recipients are known to be in need of legal services or not (targeted mail, at one time banned by the rules, refers to mailings, discussing specific types of legal services, sent to people known to need those services—but see timing exception below)

- direct solicitation of a family member or current or former client

- in-person telephone contact to solicit membership in a prepaid or group legal service plan operated by an organization not owned or directed by the lawyer

In some jurisdictions, there may be a requirement that written, telephone, or video solicitations contain the words "Advertising Material."

Many states impose additional regulations, such as the color of ink, the size of type, and the locations of any required labeling,[18] or time limits on when targeted direct mail can be sent, for example, not until 30 days after the incident that creates a need for the legal services.[19] Remember that because a paralegal's conduct must be compatible with the professional obligations of the employing lawyer, it would be improper for the paralegal to use any of the solicitation methods that are forbidden to the firm's lawyers.

ABA Model Rule 7.3(b) prohibits solicitation of any kind, including written solicitations, to persons who have made it known that they do not want to be solicited or to any individual when the solicitation involves coercion, duress, or harassment. Some state and federal statutes prohibit or limit other forms of communications, such as unrequested fax solicitations. In general, all forms of solicitation are subject to limitations in recognition of the fact that those who are in need of legal services are frequently in a state of trauma or stress and may not be in a position to make clear judgments about hiring a lawyer and proceeding with a legal matter. There is concern as well that lawyers, as trained advocates, may be especially persuasive in their efforts to obtain clients.

Paralegals should note that in some states there are statutes separate from the ethics rules that impose limits on solicitation. These are known as barratry statutes. They are designed to stop "ambulance chasing" and to prevent the courts from being clogged with litigation that has no merit.

Unlike the ethics provisions, which only apply to lawyers, barratry statutes are criminal laws that can be enforced against anyone accused of violating them. Therefore, any paralegal who is involved in the marketing of legal services should make a point of knowing those statutes as well as the applicable ethics provisions.

◆ OTHER ADVERTISING AND MARKETING REGULATIONS

In addition to the prohibition against false and misleading communications and limits on solicitation, each state may have a variety of other regulations governing lawyer advertising and solicitation. Provisions limit, regulate, and sometimes prohibit the use of dramatizations, illustrations, music, and actors, as well as regulate disclaimers, disclosures, and referral activities.

Several states require law firms to retain copies of their advertisements for a specified number of years. Some states require lawyers to file copies of their advertising and solicitation materials, and a few require lawyers to submit their advertisements to a state board for the purpose of screening them to ensure compliance with the state's rules.[20]

It is important for both lawyers and paralegals to understand that the rules must be researched in order for a law firm to comply fully with all of the required provisions. Rarely will the application of common sense be sufficient to result in absolute compliance, even for the most distinguished and dignified marketing endeavors.

◆ MULTISTATE MARKETING PROBLEMS

Even though the rules governing lawyers vary from state to state, most forms of marketing and advertising reach beyond state lines. Brochures, newsletters, and direct mail solicitation letters frequently are interstate communications. Television and radio commercials may be local, but often appear in several jurisdictions. This raises the question of multistate compliance: does a law firm that is advertising in other states have to comply with the rules where the potential clients reside or only with the rules of the state where the law office is located?

The problem of multistate compliance is especially difficult with the use of new technologies and the emergence of the Internet as a marketing tool for legal services. In that situation, the technology has no geographic limit at all. Does the law firm need to comply with the rules of every state?

It is clear that a law firm must comply with the rules of each state in which a member of the firm is admitted to practice. If it fails to do so, the lawyer who is admitted to practice in the state where the advertising does not comply with the rules could be subject to disciplinary action.

However, a law firm's website and other Internet communications present a somewhat different issue because the information is available for anyone, located anywhere, to see. The ABA has issued an ethics opinion that makes it clear that the false and misleading standard applies to websites.[21] State ethics opinions have advised lawyers to show on their websites the jurisdictions where they are admitted to practice to make clear the geographic limitations of the lawyer's practice.[22]

New multijurisdictional practice rules may help to define the limits of lawyers' interstate marketing practices. In 2002, the ABA amended Model Rule 5.5, which prohibits lawyers not admitted in a particular jurisdiction from "holding themselves out to the public as if they were admitted to practice [in that jurisdiction]."[23] Therefore, it would appear that, under this rule, lawyers may not disseminate into a jurisdiction marketing materials that would give the false impression to the public that the lawyer is licensed to practice law in that jurisdiction. Such a false impression may be created by express statements or by the omission of facts that are necessary to make the advertisement not materially misleading.[24]

◆ USING THE INTERNET

In addition to the multistate practice issues surrounding advertising over the Internet, the issue of privacy rights has arisen and been addressed by a few states. For instance, the Hearing Committee of the Tennessee Board of Professional Responsibility found that a lawyer who sent a junk-mail-like posting of an advertising message to thousands of Internet groups and lists (called "spamming") had violated the state's ethics rules.[25]

The hearing committee noted that the message did not include the mandatory notice that it was an advertisement and did not contain a required disclaimer regarding specialization. In addition, a copy of the message was not given to the Board of Professional Responsibility as required. These are issues that would arise in any kind of written advertising. Another state, Ohio, has also advised lawyers that e-mails must comply with lawyer advertising rules, including those on targeted direct mail, and must not violate federal and state laws regulating unsolicited commercial e-mail.[26] However, it is not yet clear whether every jurisdiction will treat messages over the Internet as written communications or as in-person or live contacts. Because the advertising rules differ as to what is allowable under these different types of communication, the decision as to how Internet messages will be classified will affect how the technology may be used ethically.

CHAPTER SUMMARY

- All law firm marketing activities are subject to the ethics rules.

- The most fundamental regulation governing lawyer advertising and legal services marketing is the prohibition against false or misleading communications.

- If a paralegal is asked to input, proofread, or review marketing materials, he or she should take extra care to ensure that there is nothing false or misleading.

- Some states have disapproved of including the names of nonlawyers on letterhead.

- It is essential that staff titles be included on letterhead and business cards in ways that are prominent and make the status of the staff clear and unambiguous.

- If a paralegal does not properly identify himself or herself when signing correspondence on firm letterhead, he or she may run the risk of being accused of the unauthorized practice of law.

- It is improper for a paralegal to use any of the solicitation methods that are forbidden to the firm's lawyers.

- There is no clear consensus regarding the regulation of advertising over the Internet. A paralegal assigned to work on Internet communications should be aware of recent opinions and developments in this area and should remember to comply with all the jurisdiction's rules regarding advertising.

♦ Notes

1. Bates v. State Bar of Ariz., 433 U.S. 350 (1977).
2. ABA Canons of Prof'l Ethics Canon 27 (1908).
3. *Professionalism & Ethics in Lawyer Advertising*, ABA, http://www.americanbar.org/groups/professional_responsibility/resources/professionalism/professionalism_ethics_in_lawyer_advertising.html (last visited Apr. 10, 2015).
4. Zauderer v. Office of Disciplinary Counsel, 471 U.S. 626 (1985) (lawyer may not be disciplined for soliciting legal business through printed advertising containing truthful and non-deceptive information and advice regarding legal rights of potential clients); *see also* Shapero v. Ky. Bar Ass'n, 486 U.S. 466 (1988) (state could not categorically prohibit lawyers from soliciting legal business for pecuniary gain by sending truthful and non-deceptive letters to potential clients).
5. *Zauderer*, 471 U.S. at 653 (state requirement that advertisement for services on contingent fee basis must state that unsuccessful litigant may be liable for court costs is reasonably related to substantial state interest).
6. Laws. Man. on Prof. Conduct (ABA/BNA) 81:302 (Dec. 18, 2013).
7. *See In re* Coale, 775 N.E.2d 1079 (Ind. 2002) (lawyer sent advertising materials to plane-crash victims and their relatives containing statement that lawyers "helped other victims 'through [their] tragedy and winning for them substantial compensation for their tragic loss.'"); Attorney Grievance Comm'n v. McCloskey, 511 A.2d 56 (Md. 1986) (nationwide advertisement offering "quickie divorce" created unjustified expectation); Ohio Supreme Court Ethics Op. 2002-7 (2002) (advertisement that lists settlement or verdict amounts obtained in past cases, such as "Trip/Fall sidewalk-brain injury, $1,000,000 verdict," create unjustified expectation about results lawyer can achieve).
8. *See* Florida Bar: Petition to Amend the Rules Regulating the Florida Bar—Advertising Issues, 571 So. 2d 451 (Fla. 1991) (Florida bans testimonials or endorsements of any kind as "inherently misleading," causing potential clients to "infer from the testimonial that the lawyer will reach similar results in future cases"); *In re* Keller, 792 N.E.2d 865 (Ind. 2003) (television commercial that stated that insurance companies will settle cases based on law firm's name contained an impermissible implied endorsement of firm); Conn. Bar Ass'n Comm. on Prof'l Ethics, Informal Op. 88-3 (1988) (lawyer may not circulate article with client endorsement); Ohio Supreme Court Ethics Op. 2000-6 (2000) (advertisements containing client testimonials are not permitted under the Ohio Code of Professional Responsibility).
9. Spencer v. Honorable Justices of the Supreme Court of Pa., 579 F. Supp. 880 (E.D. Pa. 1984), *aff'd*, 760 F.2d 261 (3d Cir. 1985) (subjective terms such as "experienced," "expert," "highly qualified," or "competent" are difficult to verify and may be banned). Prof'l Guidance Comm., Phil. Bar Ass'n Op. 88-18 (1988) (unverifiable characterizations such as "good lawyer" should be avoided); Prof'l

Guidance Comm., Phil. Bar Ass'n Op. 86-11 (1986) (lawyer cannot use term "experienced," "reputable," or "efficient").

10. See, for example, AVVO, Best Lawyers, Martindale-Hubbell, Super Lawyers.

11. *See, e.g.*, State Bar of Ariz. Ethics Op. 05-03 (Advertising); N.C. State Bar 2007 Formal Ethics Op. 14.

12. *In re* Foster, 45 So. 3d 1026 (La. 2010).

13. Conn. Bar Ass'n Comm. on Prof'l Ethics, Informal Op. 83-3 (1983) (lawyers admitted in different states may form partnerships and include both lawyers' names in the firm name; letterhead and other listings must indicate their jurisdictional limitations); Utah State Bar Ethics Advisory Op. Comm. Op. 96-14 (1996) (identification of the lawyers in any office of the firm must include the jurisdictional limitations on those not licensed to practice in the jurisdiction where the office is located).

14. *See* MODEL RULES OF PROF'L CONDUCT R. 7.5(c) (2013).

15. Knapp v. State Bar, No. 76-2008-F (Tex. Dist. Ct. Nueces Cnty. Aug. 5, 1977) (unreported) ("Law Center" improper name for office of sole practitioner).

16. See NFPA Informal Ethics and Disciplinary Opinion No. 2000-1 for a discussion of whether paralegals may advertise as to their certification.

17. In New Hampshire, a paralegal's name may not be included on the letterhead of a lawyer or law firm. However, a paralegal may have a business card with the firm name appearing on it provided the nonlawyer status of the paralegal is clearly disclosed. The business card is designed to identify the paralegal and to state by whom the paralegal is employed. *See* N.H. R. SUP. CT. R. 35.

18. Arizona requires that lawyers who send targeted solicitation letters send a copy to the clerk of the Arizona Supreme Court and also to the state bar. Further, the communication must include the words "Advertising Material" in twice the font size of the body of the communication on the outside envelope, if any, and at the beginning and end of the communication. ARIZ. R. SUP. CT. R. 42, ER 7.3 (2003).

19. Fla. Bar v. Went for It, 115 S. Ct. 2371 (1995).

20. Connecticut, Maryland, and New Jersey require lawyers to keep copies or recordings of advertisements for three years with record of when and where used. In New Jersey, television advertisements may not contain drawings, animations, dramatization, music, or lyrics.

21. ABA Comm. on Ethics & Prof'l Responsibility, Formal Op. 457 (2010).

22. *See, e.g.*, Cal. Ethics Op. 2001-155 (2001) (advising California lawyers using websites to assure themselves that they are complying with any applicable rules of the different jurisdictions involved, including rules governing the unauthorized practice of law; alternatively, they can take steps to make clear that they are not advertising in other jurisdictions); N.Y. State Ethics Op. 709 (1998) ("any Internet advertisement should inform a potential client of the jurisdiction in which the attorney is licensed, and should not mislead the potential client into believing that the attorney is licensed in a jurisdiction where the attorney is not licensed").

23. Almost every jurisdiction has adopted a version of this rule that is the same or similar to the ABA Model Rule.

24. *See* MODEL RULES OF PROF'L CONDUCT R. 7.1 (2013).

25. *In re* Canter, No. 95-831-O-H (Tenn. Bd. of Prof. Resp. Feb. 25, 1997).

26. *See* Ohio Supreme Court Bd. of Comm'rs on Grievances & Discipline, Op. 2004-1 (2004) (advising that e-mails must comply with lawyer advertising rules, including those on targeted direct mail, and must not violate federal and state laws regulating unsolicited commercial e-mail).

Chapter TEN

Legal Fees and Employee Compensation

▶ A competent paralegal can be crucial to an efficient system of billing and collection. For example, when a law firm is seeking legal fees from an adversary after extended litigation, fees to be approved by the court are dependent on the preparation of a comprehensive and thorough fee petition that honestly sets forth the legal services performed for the client.

Although paralegals are not permitted to establish the fee to be charged for a legal service[1] or directly share in the fees, they often have responsibility for preparing and documenting detailed financial records, including billing statements.

For most lawyers, creation of fee agreements, careful and efficient billing procedures, and responsible handling of employee compensation matters are critical to successful practice. Absent appropriate attention to these details, lawyers may find themselves in a constant struggle to make ends meet, have a parade of disgruntled clients, and even have a raft of inquiries from the local disciplinary agency. It is important for the paralegal to understand the rules on legal fees and employee compensation outlined below, both to handle assigned fee matters properly and to avoid missteps that can create difficulties for the paralegal, the lawyer, and the clients.

▶ Fee Agreements

Client representations are best begun with a clear, written understanding of the legal fees involved. A fee agreement allows a lawyer and client to make clear from the inception of the legal representation the scope of that representation and the basis for the compensation of the lawyer and his or her staff. A clearly drafted agreement that is fully explained to the client at the time the representation begins will minimize disagreements as the representation proceeds and assist in resolving any disputes that may arise when the representation ends.

The paralegal who is involved in the preparation of a written fee agreement should make certain that the lawyer has given instructions regarding all the relevant items listed in the box "What Should the Fee Agreement Cover?" (page 123). But, as stated in Canon 3 of the National Association for Legal Assistants (NALA) Code of Ethics and Professional Responsibility, a paralegal shall not engage in the practice of law by setting legal fees.

Every representation must have some form of fee agreement. ABA Model Rule of Professional Conduct 1.5(b) states that the scope of the representation and the basis or rate of the fee and expenses must be communicated to the client before or within a reasonable time after the representation commences. Furthermore, any changes to an existing fee arrangement or to a lawyer's regular hourly billing rates must be properly communicated to the client and be reasonable under the circumstances.[2]

While there is no requirement in the ABA Model Rules that all fee agreements be in writing, and oral fee agreements may be enforceable in certain types of matters, Model Rule 1.5(b) does state a preference that fee agreements be in writing, except when the lawyer is charging a regularly represented client on the same basis or rate. If the amount of the fee is contingent upon the success of or monetary recovery in a particular representation, the agreement must be in writing.

With the informed consent of a client, contingent fee agreements are permitted in a variety of situations and are not limited to personal injury or litigation matters.[3] However, Model Rule 1.5(d) prohibits the use of contingent fee agreements in domestic relations and criminal matters.

There are some jurisdictions that mandate the use of written fee agreements more extensively than is required by Model Rule 1.5. For example, several jurisdictions require that the fee agreement be in writing whenever the lawyer has not regularly represented the client.[4]

Prior to entering into the fee agreement, lawyers have an obligation to discuss payment options with the client.[5] The fee agreement between the lawyer and client should set forth both the basis and method for payment of the lawyer's fee. It should also set forth the details of the client's and lawyer's expectations as to the nature and scope of the representation.

▸ BILLING/COLLECTION[6]

EC-1.2(c) of the National Federation of Paralegal Associations (NFPA) Model Code of Ethics and Professional Responsibility states that "[a] paralegal shall ensure that all timekeeping and billing records prepared by the paralegal are thorough, accurate, honest, and complete."

There are numerous billing situations that arise in a busy law practice that involve more than just counting hours and must be dealt with carefully. For example, a lawyer may not bill more than one client for the same hours worked by charging a client for the time it took to produce a document that the lawyer had already created for another client. The lawyer also is prohibited from charging two clients for the same hours when the lawyer works on one client's matter while traveling for the benefit of the other client on a different matter.[7]

Reasonableness of Fees

▼ By specific prohibition of Model Rule 1.5 (Fees), lawyers may not enter into an agreement for, charge, or collect an unreasonable fee. While reasonableness is not defined, and the reasonableness of a particular fee will be dependent on the unique circumstances of the representation, the rule identifies eight factors that may be taken into account:

► the time and labor required, the novelty and difficulty of the questions involved, and the skill requisite to perform the legal service properly

► the likelihood, if apparent to the client, that the acceptance of the particular employment will preclude other employment by the lawyer

► the fee customarily charged in the locality for similar legal services

► the amount involved and the results obtained

► the time limitations imposed by the client or by the circumstances

► the nature and length of the professional relationship with the client

► the experience, reputation, and ability of the lawyer or lawyers performing the services

► whether the fee is fixed or contingent

Lawyers must be careful to bill clients according to the correct agreed-upon rate for the services performed. In almost all circumstances, a paralegal's time would not be billed at the lawyer's hourly rate. As discussed in Chapter 1, while paralegals are capable of carrying out many substantive duties that would be billed at a higher rate if performed by a lawyer, the U.S. Supreme Court has allowed a separate compensation award for paralegals and law clerks performing these tasks.

> **What Should the Fee Agreement Cover?**
>
> ▼ The fee agreement should cover the following:
> - the identity of the client or clients to be represented
> - the full extent of the services to be performed
> - the limitations, if any, to be placed on the services to be performed
> - the nature of the lawyer's compensation, hourly fee, contingent, or other arrangement, and how the client will be billed
> - the hourly rate to be charged by every lawyer or paralegal who will be working on the matter
> - how often the client will be billed, whether interest or a finance charge must be paid, and when payment is expected
> - how the lawyer is to be compensated if the lawyer is discharged before completing the representation
> - the charges for travel time, costs, and other expenses
> - whether expenses are to be deducted before or after the contingent fee is calculated in a contingent fee agreement

A paralegal's services may be billed at "market rate" rather than the "actual cost" to the lawyer.[8] Note, however, that charges for work performed by paralegals may be reduced or disallowed if the work was secretarial in nature; that is, work that lawyers traditionally would not have performed.[9] With more and more lawyers drafting documents on their computers, this may be an increasingly difficult standard to assess.

Sometimes law firms hire lawyers from outside the firm to work on a contract basis on particular client matters. The costs associated with the contract may be billed to the client either as legal fees or as business expenses. If they are billed as business expenses, the client may be billed only the actual costs, unless the client agrees otherwise. On the other hand, if the costs are billed as legal fees, then a surcharge may be added as long as the total fee is still reasonable.[10]

Other charges related to the representation also must be reasonable.[11] Thus, for example, in regard to travel expenses incurred on behalf of the client, it would be improper for the lawyer to charge the client an amount in excess of the lawyer's actual costs. A paralegal who has the responsibility of compiling and billing expenses for reimbursement from the client must comply with this restriction.

Specific charges for in-house services such as photocopying or messengering documents may be agreed upon in advance with the client, but, if not, should not exceed actual costs plus a reasonable allocation of overhead expenses directly associated with the provision of the services. The paralegal who prepares bills including such charges must be aware of any agreement with the client and the standard rate charged by the firm in the absence of an agreement.

If a dispute over the billing or collection of fees does arise, lawyers should attempt to resolve the matter using established procedures for the resolution of fee disputes.[12] The ABA Standing Committee on Client Protection has developed Model Rules for Fee Arbitration, and there are at least 12 jurisdictions that have made fee arbitration mandatory if the client requests it.[13]

One frequently arising dispute is whether a particular sum of money paid by a client to the lawyer was a retainer or an advance, and, thus, whether the money is refundable if not earned prior to the conclusion of the representation or discharge of the lawyer. A true retainer is an amount paid by the client to the lawyer, not for specific services but, rather, to ensure the lawyer's availability whenever the client may need legal representation. An advance payment made by a client to a lawyer is for specific legal representation and the accompanying expenses. A true retainer may be non-refundable. An advance payment may be at least partially refundable if the client terminates the services of the lawyer prior to the completion of the representation. Since a true retainer is considered earned when paid, it should be deposited into the lawyer's general business account or operating account.

While there is some difference between jurisdictions, the general rule is that an advance payment is not earned until the services are performed and should be deposited into a client trust account or IOLTA (Interest on Lawyers Trust Accounts) (see Chapter 11) and withdrawn only in part as earned. When such a withdrawal is made, the client should be notified of the hours billed, the amount withdrawn, and the balance remaining in the account.

The paralegal who is handling funds on behalf of a lawyer must be sure to get specific instructions from the lawyer as to what accounts are to be used for what funds.

Finally, ABA Model Rule 1.16(d) states that when a lawyer has been discharged, the lawyer shall take all necessary steps to protect the interests of the client, including refunding any portion of an advance payment that has not been earned.

◆ Sharing Fees

ABA Model Rule 1.5(e) permits two or more lawyers who are not in the same firm to divide a fee if either "the division is in proportion to the services performed by each lawyer or each lawyer assumes joint responsibility for the representation." In addition, the client must agree to the arrangement, the arrangement must be confirmed in writing, and the total fee must be reasonable.

Model Rule 5.4(a) prohibits a lawyer or law firm from sharing fees with someone who is not a lawyer, except when dealing with the estate of a deceased, disabled, or disappeared lawyer, or establishing compensation or retirement plans for nonlawyer employees. A lawyer may also share court-awarded legal fees with nonprofit organizations that employ, retain, or recommend the lawyer's employment in the matter. The rationale for the general prohibition is that fee splitting between a lawyer and a layperson could interfere with the lawyer's professional judgment and could lead to control by a layperson only concerned with profit and not the interests of the client.[14]

Although the rule applies to many situations, its significance for the paralegal most likely arises when he or she refers a friend, relative, or acquaintance to the firm for representation. The lawyer is not permitted to share the fee generated from the representation with the paralegal or to pay the paralegal a bonus for bringing in the client. However, the paralegal's compensation may be based upon a percentage of the law firm's gross or net income provided that it is not tied to specific fees from a particular case.[15]

Moreover, there is no general rule that prohibits a lawyer from paying a paralegal a discretionary bonus, not based upon the generation of specific fees, when, for example, the lawyer has had a particularly successful year. However, some jurisdictions do place restrictions on the terms of bonuses paid to paralegals. For example, in Georgia, it is ethically improper to pay paralegals a monthly bonus based upon the gross receipts of the law office. In Florida, a lawyer may not give a bonus to a nonlawyer employee solely based on the number of hours worked by the employee.[16]

CHAPTER SUMMARY

- [✓] Lawyers may not charge unreasonable fees or costs.
- [✓] Two clients may not be billed for the same time.
- [✓] Every representation must have some form of fee agreement.
- [✓] A paralegal may not set legal fees.
- [✓] A paralegal handling funds for a lawyer must be careful to make deposits to and withdrawals from the proper accounts.
- [✓] A paralegal may not share in legal fees or be paid a bonus for bringing in a client.

NOTES

1. *See* ABA MODEL GUIDELINES FOR THE UTILIZATION OF PARALEGAL SERVICES Guideline 3 (2012); NALA CODE OF ETHICS AND PROFESSIONAL RESPONSIBILITY Canon 3 (2007).
2. ABA Comm. on Ethics & Prof'l Responsibility, Formal Op. 458 (2011).

3. ABA Comm. on Ethics & Prof'l Responsibility, Formal Op. 389 (1994).

4. For example, Connecticut, the District of Columbia, New Jersey, and Pennsylvania.

5. ABA Comm. on Ethics & Prof'l Responsibility, Formal Op. 389 (1994).

6. *See Time & Billing Software*, ABA LEGAL TECH. RESOURCE CTR., http://www.americanbar.org/groups/departments_offices/legal_technology_resources/resources/charts_fyis/timeandbilling.html for information on time and billing software (last visited Apr. 13, 2015).

7. ABA Comm. on Ethics & Prof'l Responsibility, Formal Op. 379 (1993).

8. Richlin Sec. Serv. Co. v. Chertoff, 553 U.S. 571 (2008). It is not permissible to bill the paralegal as an expert. *See* Emery v. Hunt, 132 F. Supp. 2d 803 (D.S.D. 2001), *aff'd by* 272 F.3d 1042 (8th Cir. 2001).

9. *See, e.g.*, *In re* Busy Beaver, 19 F.3d 833 (3d Cir. 1994) (bankruptcy statute specifies that the type of service performed by a paralegal, including whether it is clerical, affects the rate of compensation).

10. ABA Comm. on Ethics & Prof'l Responsibility, Formal Op. 420 (2000).

11. *Id*.

12. MODEL RULES OF PROF'L CONDUCT R. 1.5 cmt. 9 (2013).

13. Alaska, California, the District of Columbia, Georgia, Maine, Montana, New Jersey, New York, North Carolina, Ohio, South Carolina, and Wyoming. *See Jurisdictions with Mandatory Fee Arbitration Programs*, ABA CTR. PROF. RESP. (June 20, 2012), http://www.americanbar.org/content/dam/aba/administrative/professional_responsibility/fee_arb_chart.authcheckdam.pdf.

14. ABA Comm. on Ethics & Prof'l Responsibility, Formal Op. 355 (1987) (prohibition avoids possibility of nonlawyer's interference with exercise of lawyer's independent professional judgment and ensures that total fee paid by client not unreasonably high).

15. *See* D.C. Bar Legal Ethics Comm., Op. 322 (2004); Utah State Bar Ethics Advisory Op. Comm. Op. 02-07 (2002).

16. *See* Fla. Bar Prof'l Ethics Comm. Op. 02-1 (2002).

Chapter ELEVEN

Client Funds and Property

- Lawyers may be entrusted with many types of client property: escrow money paid to the lawyer in anticipation of a real estate closing, securities held pending sale, exhibits to be used as evidence during litigation, documents submitted pursuant to subpoena, and others. Regardless of what form a client's property takes, the lawyer is expected to serve as a trustworthy fiduciary while handling it. For example, a Florida lawyer was disciplined for negligence in regard to the safekeeping of a client's firearms.[1] The lawyer also has an obligation to ensure that his or her employees act properly in regard to the property.

♦ SAFEKEEPING BY THE PARALEGAL

Though a lawyer may ask the paralegal to assist, the safekeeping of client property is the sole responsibility of the lawyer.[2] If a lawyer assigns the task of balancing client trust accounts to a paralegal, the lawyer will ultimately be responsible for the maintenance and accuracy of the records and the safety of the funds. The lawyer cannot avoid disciplinary liability by claiming that the task was delegated to someone else.

However, notwithstanding the lawyer's ultimate accountability, the paralegal is never relieved of the obligation to follow safekeeping procedures. Nonlawyers can be subject to charges of negligence or criminal conversion if they cannot account for client property in their control.[3]

Accordingly, paralegals should study their jurisdiction's rules and learn how to fulfill the segregation, record keeping, and notification duties associated with client property. EC-1.2(e) of the National Federation of Paralegal Associations (NFPA) Model Code of Ethics and Professional Responsibility also addresses these obligations, requiring that a paralegal be scrupulous, thorough, and honest in identifying and maintaining a client's property.

To help avoid problems, a paralegal who is asked to work with client funds must be comfortable handling those responsibilities[4] and should ask for as much instruction or training from the lawyer as necessary regarding the ethical obligations.

In addition to responsibilities regarding financial records of the firm, paralegals may be asked to keep safe the non-monetary property of clients—for example, valuable items such as securities or client documents to be produced at trial. Because offices are not inviolable and coworkers and many others frequently have unrestricted access to them, valuables should be placed in a safe deposit box, and other property should be labeled with identifying information and safeguarded appropriately.

Because paralegals often handle the record-keeping functions of a law office, including bank deposits, and maintain the personal property of clients, they must act in a trustworthy fashion and understand the obligations imposed by ABA Model Rule of Professional Conduct 1.15 (Safekeeping Property).

The loss of client property by a paralegal can cause harm to a client and result in serious consequences, not just for the paralegal but also for the employing lawyer. These consequences may include disciplinary sanctions, charges of negligence, or even criminal charges of conversion.

▶ ABA Model Rule on Safekeeping Property

The ABA Model Rules include a critical directive on the safekeeping of property: Model Rule 1.15. This rule highlights the lawyer's obligations regarding client property.

A violation of this rule is considered one of the gravest infractions a lawyer can commit. Thus, courts have treated misappropriation of client funds as an ethical violation warranting disbarment.[5] Even inadvertent breaches frequently result in discipline by regulatory authorities. Moreover, it is no defense that the client was not harmed or that the funds were returned before they were missed.[6] The rule offers protection for clients by imposing three obligations: the lawyer must segregate funds and property of clients, keep careful and correct financial records, and make timely notification to clients of the receipt of funds on their behalf.

Segregation of Funds and Property

A lawyer who combines his or her own money with the money of one or more of his or her clients is said to have "commingled" funds, which is specifically prohibited under Model Rule 1.15. The rule requires lawyers to segregate the property of clients and third persons from the lawyer's own property: money must be held in one or more accounts separate from a lawyer's personal and business accounts, and property other than money must be identified as belonging to the client and appropriately safeguarded.[7] However, in 2002, Model Rule 1.15 was amended to permit a lawyer to deposit his or her own money in a client trust account in order to repay bank charges on the account. The amount deposited may not exceed the amount needed to pay back those charges.[8]

These obligations are imposed on lawyers because lawyers act in a fiduciary capacity—a position of trust—when handling the property of others.[9] When clients entrust their money or property to a lawyer, they expect that their property will be properly accounted for and, if appropriate, promptly returned.

The separate account requirement of Model Rule 1.15 ensures that client property is not confused with the lawyer's property—either by the lawyer or by the lawyer's creditors.

This becomes especially important when a creditor of a lawyer seeks to obtain the lawyer's property in satisfaction of a debt. If the lawyer has commingled personal funds with client money, the creditor might be able to obtain the client's money, as well as the lawyer's, in payment of the debt.[10] A lawyer who commingles personal and client funds is subject to discipline,[11] regardless of whether any of the client funds are ever taken for the lawyer's personal use.[12]

Table 11.1

What *must* be held in a client trust account?	What *may not* be held in a client trust account?
▶ client or third-party funds	▶ personal funds
▶ funds that belong partly to a client and partly to a lawyer (e.g., settlement funds, disputed advances for legal fees)	▶ business and investment money
▶ retainers for legal services where the retainer remains the property of the client until the work is performed	▶ fee payments that have become the lawyer's personal property

Adequate Bookkeeping

When segregating money, lawyers need not establish a separate account for each client. They may combine the funds of two or more clients into one account, provided that they keep strict records of each client's funds.[13]

If they do so, they must think of and treat each client's money as a separate account within the general client account and must balance each separate client's account.[14] It is not sufficient that the general client account balances. Separation is achieved by using a distinct ledger or balance sheet for each client. The records must show exactly which funds were deposited into the account on behalf of each client, from which source those funds came, the amount of funds withdrawn, and how withdrawn funds were used.

Model Rule 1.15 requires lawyers to maintain records of what property belongs to which client and to keep those records for five years after the representation of the client has ended. (Various jurisdictions have different time periods for record maintenance.) Lawyers also must give the client a prompt accounting of all property upon the client's request.

Some jurisdictions provide detailed information on trust account bookkeeping to help a lawyer comply with their version of Model Rule 1.15, instructing lawyers on how to track each client's money and how to balance each account within the account.[15]

Of utmost importance is the lawyer's obligation not to draw on a client's funds until the funds have completed the bank clearing process. Even though the general client account may have adequate resources, it is unethical for the lawyer to withdraw a specific client's funds until there are enough cleared funds in the account belonging to that client.[16]

Lawyers commit conversion when they use one client's funds for their own use or for that of a different client. Any unauthorized use of a client's property for a lawyer's or paralegal's personal or business use is conversion.[17] The unauthorized use can be temporary, and the lawyer or paralegal need not derive any gain or benefit from the use in order for the conduct to be sanctionable.[18]

A lawyer may find it tempting to "borrow" from one client's part of the trust account to accommodate another, favored client. The lawyer may reason that if there is sufficient money in the general client trust account, the check won't bounce because the first client's money will act as a cushion; then the "borrowed" funds will be automatically replaced when the favored client's check clears.

The first client's money will, in fact, prevent the check from bouncing, but the lawyer will have committed conversion nonetheless. Each client's account balance within the general trust account must never drop below zero.

Another common way for a lawyer to convert client property is to spend client money that has been deposited in the lawyer's personal or business accounts.[19] Conversion may occur even when lawyers withdraw client funds believing that they are entitled to them.

However, as the comment to Model Rule 1.15 explains, a lawyer may withdraw funds from a client trust account for the lawyer's own use if the client has entered into a prepaid fee arrangement. In such an arrangement, the client pays in advance for legal work to be performed, and the lawyer is entitled to make withdrawals as the fee is earned.

Financial Records

Model Rule 1.15(a) requires lawyers to maintain "complete records" regarding a lawyer's trust or escrow accounts, but it does not provide lawyers with practical guidance in complying with these record-keeping duties.

In 1993, the ABA House of Delegates approved the Model Financial Recordkeeping Rule, which delineated the types of documents that must be maintained by a lawyer during his or her practice as well as at the sale or

Paper Trail of Actions Taken in a Typical Transaction

▼ Accountability requires that all aspects of the transaction be traceable from the time of receipt of the funds, up to and including the disbursement of the funds by check, proper negotiation of that check by the payee, and clearance through the banking process. In the typical transaction, where the client gives money to the lawyer, who then deposits it in the client trust account and pays the money out at the direction of the client, the following documents would provide a paper trail for the lawyer of what actions were taken:

► the initial deposit slip or copy of a bank receipt, which would show the date of deposit, the amount of deposit, the name of the client on whose behalf the money has been received, the source of the funds, and the date stamp showing the date the deposit was received by the bank;

► the bank statement, which would show that the bank credited the deposit and when it was credited;

Client Funds and Property 135

dissolution of the practice. That rule was replaced in 2010 by the Model Rules for Client Trust Account Records (see Appendix F).

Quite a few jurisdictions have adopted their own financial record-keeping rules.[20] Lawyers may be disciplined for failing to follow these rules. Some jurisdictions provide detailed information on trust account bookkeeping, such as how to track each client's money and how to balance each account within the account.[21]

Proper Notification

Sometimes a lawyer obtains property belonging to a client from a source other than the client, such as settlement proceeds from the sale of a house. At other times, the lawyer holds property the client wants returned. For example, clients often want their files returned when legal representation is

---

Continued from previous page

▶ the checkbook stub, which would show when disbursements were made and to whom;

▶ the disbursement check, which would show the date it was drawn, the amount and the name of the payee, the purpose of the check, the order of negotiation (from the endorsements), and the date deposited for collection;

▶ the bank statement, which would show the date the trust account was actually charged for the check; and

▶ any file documentation that would explain the deposit or the authority for how the money should be distributed, such as a closing statement, a court order, or a signed authorization by the client for the disbursement of funds.

Each deposit and disbursement should describe the client and matter to which it relates.

Reprinted with permission of the Attorney Registration and Disciplinary Commission of the Supreme Court of Illinois.

completed. In circumstances such as these, the ABA Model Rules work to protect client property through notification requirements. Model Rule 1.15 requires a lawyer to notify a client of the receipt of property and to deliver it promptly if the client is entitled to the property. Failure to do so can result in disciplinary action.[22]

Additional protections are to be found in the ABA's Model Rule for Trust Account Overdraft Notification and Model Rule for Payee Notification, both of which are more procedural rules than they are ethical rules.

The overdraft rule requires financial institutions handling lawyer trust accounts to notify appropriate lawyer discipline offices when they dishonor

Client Subsidiary Ledger Page

▼ This ledger records chronologically for each client or third person for whom funds are held in trust all receipts, disbursements, and balances. Without a subsidiary ledger the lawyer would likely be unable to know the amount of funds that must be maintained for a given client or third person and to provide an accurate and complete accounting on request. Also, the FDIC insurance rules require that to fully insure each client's or third person's funds being held in the Interest on Lawyer Trust Account (IOLTA) client trust account, each client and third person's interests must be ascertainable from the client trust account records. Each subsidiary ledger would include:

▶ Separate subsidiary ledger pages for each client or third person for whom funds are held in trust.

▶ Posting transactions (receipts and disbursements) by date, purpose and amount.

▶ If the client trust account is opened for the benefit of one client or third person or if the account allocates interest to each client or third person, any net interest (accrued interest less service charges) credited to the client or third person.

Reprinted with permission of the Attorney Registration and Disciplinary Commission of the Supreme Court of Illinois.

> **Trust Account Client Ledger Page**
>
> - Name of Client: _____
> - Legal Matter/Adverse Party: _____
> - File or Case Number: _____

> **Trust Account Checkbook Register**
>
> A client trust account checkbook register is like any other checkbook register. It is used to record deposits and client trust account checks in sequential order and is also used to maintain a running balance. To properly maintain the checkbook register, check stubs, bank statements, records of deposit, and checks or other records of debits must also be maintained.
>
> *Boxes on this page reprinted with permission of the Attorney Registration and Disciplinary Commission of the Supreme Court of Illinois.*

a lawyer's drafts from client trust accounts for insufficient funds. This enables the authorities to intervene before major losses occur and significant numbers of clients are harmed; errant lawyers can be encouraged or required to take corrective action before their misconduct has become so egregious as to mandate serious sanction. Participation by financial institutions is a prerequisite to their eligibility to hold lawyer trust accounts.

The payee notification rule is designed to protect against a variety of misconduct by a lawyer involved in the settlement of a client's claim: unauthorized settlement with the defendant's insurer, forgery of the claimant's signature on a stipulation of settlement, forgery of the claimant's endorsement on the settlement draft itself, or misappropriation of the claimant's share of the proceeds.

Such misconduct is made possible because insurance carriers typically do not notify the claimant when making payment to the lawyer or other representative of an insured. Instead, they deliver settlement proceeds in payment of liability claims to the lawyer of record for the claimant by a check made payable jointly to the claimant and the claimant's lawyer.

Written notice directly from the insurer, as is provided under the notification rule, provides the claimant with an independent and verifiable source of information concerning the facts of the settlement. It also provides the adverse party and insurer with certainty that the settlement has been concluded in a lawful manner. Thus, it helps to ensure against a lawyer's concealing any unauthorized settlement and misappropriation of funds, a situation that might otherwise go undiscovered for a considerable time and come to light at a point when the lawyer is unable to replace the misappropriated funds.

◆ Disputes about Client Funds

When a lawyer holds money in which both the lawyer and the client claim an interest—for example, when the lawyer wishes to be paid from money a client advanced as legal fees, but the client contends that the lawyer did not do the work—Model Rule 1.15 requires that the lawyer keep the disputed funds in a trust account separate from all other personal and business accounts until the dispute is resolved.

A lawyer has a duty similarly to segregate funds if a client's creditor claims an interest in the money. If there is a concern that the client will divert the money without paying the creditor, the lawyer may refuse to give the money to the client. However, the lawyer is ordinarily under no duty to turn the funds over to the creditor, even if the lawyer knows that the client rightfully owes the debt.[23] The lawyer's obligation is to segregate the disputed funds until the dispute is resolved and the lawyer is instructed to deliver the funds either by agreement of all parties or by court order.

Mishandling Client Property Can Lead to Trouble

In re Grubbs[24] demonstrates the danger of mishandling an unusual form of client property, a piece of jewelry. In *Grubbs*, a client gave his lawyer a ring valued at over $24,000 as security for payment of a $500 non-refundable retainer. Shortly after receiving the ring, Grubbs withdrew from the representation, but he did not return the ring.

Initially, he placed it in a locked box in his office, but he soon became accustomed to taking the ring with him when he left the office. He took it home to show his wife, and he carried it around while he considered having it appraised. One night, Grubbs left work with the ring, visited a tavern, spent the night at home, and returned to work the next day. When he checked his pocket, the ring was gone.

Despite repeated requests from the former client for the return of the ring in exchange for $500 cash, Grubbs refused to tell his client what had happened to the ring. After admitting the loss, Grubbs was found guilty of violations of the rule regarding safekeeping of client property and the rule against deceit and dishonesty and was reprimanded for his misconduct.

◆ INTEREST ON LAWYER TRUST ACCOUNTS

Sometimes the amount of money that a lawyer handles for a single client is quite small or to be held for only a short period of time. Traditionally, because ethical provisions prohibit lawyers from deriving any financial benefit from funds belonging to their clients, lawyers placed such funds in combined, or pooled, trust checking accounts that contained other nominal or short-term funds, earning no interest on them.

In the 1980s, when banks began paying interest on checking accounts, state laws and supreme court rules created Interest on Lawyer Trust Account (IOLTA) programs, under the provisions of which lawyers who handle nominal or short-term client funds may place them in a single, pooled, interest-bearing trust account. The financial institutions holding the accounts then forward the interest earned on the accounts to the state's IOLTA program, which most commonly uses the earnings to fund legal services for those who cannot afford them. IOLTA plans have faced constitutional challenges, but the U.S. Supreme Court recently held that Washington State's IOLTA plan does not violate the Fifth Amendment because it serves a "public use" by funding legal services for the needy and does not constitute a "regulatory taking" because clients suffer no net loss.[25]

Lawyers' Fund for Client Protection

Almost every jurisdiction in the country has a fund from which clients can be at least partially reimbursed when they have lost money or property through the dishonest conduct of a lawyer.[26] Commonly known as client protection funds, they are underwritten by voluntary or, in some cases, mandatory contributions of lawyers, though some jurisdictions draw client protection funds from general budget appropriations.[27] The amount of money reimbursed varies from jurisdiction to jurisdiction.[28]

Random Audit of Trust Accounts

Clients who have had funds stolen by a lawyer often choose not to report the theft to disciplinary authorities because they are negotiating with the lawyer for the return of their money. In such circumstances, disciplinary authorities are unaware of lawyer thefts, and, as the lawyer who has stolen money from one client steals from another to repay the first, more and more clients suffer harm. The ABA has adopted a Model Rule for Random Audit of Trust Accounts that identifies procedures for randomly selecting and auditing lawyer or law firm trust accounts. Such audits are a proven deterrent to the misuse of money and property.[29] This examination of trust accounts by court-paid auditors has the added benefit of providing lawyers with expert and practical assistance in maintaining necessary records of their accounts.

An audit usually begins with the issuance of an investigative subpoena compelling production of the records relating to a lawyer's or law firm's trust accounts. All records produced for an audit should remain confidential, and their contents should not be disclosed in violation of the attorney-client privilege.

The ABA Model Rule for Random Audit of Trust Accounts states that a lawyer or law firm should cooperate in an audit and should answer all questions pertaining to it, unless the lawyer or law firm claims a privilege or right that is available to the lawyer or law firm under applicable state or federal law. A lawyer's or law firm's failure to cooperate in an audit should constitute professional misconduct. The rule suggests that no lawyer or law firm should be subject to a random audit more frequently than once every three years. If your law firm is the subject of a random audit, a paralegal must cooperate with the officials conducting the audit, answering questions and providing information as required. However, if the paralegal's supervising lawyer claims that certain information being requested is privileged and thus should not be revealed to the auditors, the paralegal should follow the lawyer's instructions until such time as a court rules on the lawyer's claim.

Trust account overdraft notification, record keeping, and random audit rules such as those discussed above have been enacted in enough states for a sufficient time to judge their efficacy and any problems they might cause practitioners. The rules have proven effective to deter and detect the theft of funds even before clients file complaints,[30] have provided useful guidance on proper accounting procedures, and do not appear to create an undue regulatory burden on honest practitioners.

CHAPTER SUMMARY

- ☑ The paralegal must understand the obligations imposed by his or her jurisdiction's rule on the safekeeping of property.

- ☑ Paralegals should study their jurisdiction's rules and learn how to fulfill the segregation, record-keeping, and notification duties associated with client property.

- ☑ The paralegal may face civil or criminal repercussions for failure to handle client funds appropriately.

- ☑ A lawyer who commingles personal and client funds is subject to discipline regardless of whether any of the client funds are ever taken for the lawyer's personal use.

▶ NOTES

1. Fla. Bar v. Grosso, 760 So. 2d 940 (Fla. 2000).
2. CLIENT TRUST ACCOUNT HANDBOOK: A GUIDE TO CREATING AND MAINTAINING CLIENT TRUST ACCOUNTS (Attorney Registration & Disciplinary Comm'n of the Supreme Court of Ill. 2011) [hereinafter CLIENT TRUST ACCOUNT HANDBOOK], *available at* http://www.iardc.org/toc_main.html.

3. *See, e.g.*, Attorney Grievance v. Zuckerman, 872 A.2d 693 (Md. 2005) (lawyer delegated authority to paralegal to write checks on trust account; paralegal stole money from the account and upon pleading guilty to criminal charges was ordered to pay restitution and was sentenced to ten years incarceration, with seven of the years suspended).

4. See *In re David*, 690 S.E.2d 579 (S.C. 2010), for an example of a situation in which a lawyer assigned financial duties to an employee who didn't have the requisite knowledge.

5. Laws. Man. on Prof. Conduct (ABA/BNA) 45:503 (Jan. 24, 2007).

6. ELLEN J. BENNETT, ELIZABETH J. COHEN & HELEN GUNNARSSON, ANNOTATED MODEL RULES OF PROF'L CONDUCT 244 (8th ed. 2015).

7. MODEL RULES OF PROF'L CONDUCT R. 1.15(a) (2013).

8. MODEL RULES OF PROF'L CONDUCT R. 1.15(b) (2013).

9. *Id.* cmt. 1.

10. Laws. Man. on Prof. Conduct, *supra* note 5, at 45:503.

11. *Id.*

12. *Id.*

13. *Id.* at 45:501.

14. N.C. State Bar v. Sheffield, 326 S.E.2d 320 (N.C. Ct. App. 1985); CLIENT TRUST ACCOUNT HANDBOOK, *supra* note 2.

15. *See, e.g.*, *Random Audits*, N.J. JUDICIARY, http://www.judiciary.state.nj.us/oae/rap/rap.htm (last visited Apr. 13, 2015); N.C. STATE BAR, LAWYER'S TRUST ACCOUNT HANDBOOK (rev. 2014), *available at* http://www.ncbar.gov/PDFs/Trust%20Account%20Handbook.pdf; WASH. STATE BAR ASS'N, MANAGING CLIENT TRUST ACCOUNTS: RULES, REGULATIONS, AND COMMON SENSE (rev. 2013), *available at* http://wsba.org/~/media/Files/Licensing_Lawyer%20Conduct/IOLTA/Managing%20Client%20Trust%20Accounts%20September%201%202012%20lrg%20print%20with%20cover.ashx.

16. CLIENT TRUST ACCOUNT HANDBOOK, *supra* note 2; DAVID E. JOHNSON, TRUST AND BUSINESS ACCOUNTING FOR ATTORNEYS 9–12 (N.J. Inst. for Continuing Legal Educ. 1994).

17. Laws. Man. on Prof. Conduct, *supra* note 5, at 45:503.

18. *In re* Asher, 772 A.2d 1161 (D.C. 2001); *In re* Wilson, 409 A.2d 1153, 1155 n.1 (N.J. 1979).

19. BENNETT, COHEN & GUNNARSSON, *supra* note 6, at 241–42.

20. *See, e.g.*, Arizona: ARIZ. SUP. CT. RULES R. 43; California: CAL. RULES OF PROF'L CONDUCT R. 4-100; Connecticut: CONN. SUPER. CT. CIV. § 2-27 (Practice Book); Delaware: DEL. RULES OF PROF'L CONDUCT R. 1.15; Florida: RULES REGULATING THE FLA. BAR R. 5-1.1; Hawaii: HAW. RULES OF PROF'L CONDUCT R. 1.15; Illinois: ILL. SUP. CT. RULES R. 769; Iowa: IOWA SUP. CT. RULES R. 39.10; Maine: ME. BAR RULES R. 7(s); Maryland: MD. RULES OF CT. R. 16-722; Minnesota: MINN. RULES OF PROF'L CONDUCT R. 1.15(h); Montana: MONT. RULES OF CT., TRUST ACCOUNT MAINTENANCE AND AUDIT REQUIREMENTS; Nebraska: NEB. SUP. CT. RULES ON TRUST ACCTS. & BLANKET BONDS R. 3; New Jersey: N.J. RULES OF CT. R.

1:21-6; New Mexico: N.M. SUP. CT. R. 17-204; Oklahoma: OKLA. DISC. P. R. 1.4; South Dakota: S.D. CODIFIED LAWS § 16-18-20.2; Virginia: VA. RULES OF PROF'L CONDUCT R. 1.15; Washington: WASH. RULES OF PROF'L CONDUCT R. 1.14.

21. *See, e.g.*, CLIENT TRUST ACCOUNT HANDBOOK, *supra* note 2.
22. BENNETT, COHEN & GUNNARSSON, *supra* note 6, at 248.
23. *Id.* at 235–36; *see also* Alaska Bar Ass'n Ethics Comm. Op. 80-1 (1980).
24. 663 P.2d 1346 (Wash. 1983).
25. *See* Brown v. Legal Found. of Wash., 538 U.S. 216 (2003).
26. ABA SURVEY OF LAWYERS' FUNDS FOR CLIENT PROTECTION: 2008–2010 (2010), *available at* http://www.americanbar.org/content/dam/aba/administrative/professional_responsibility/29th_forum_2008_2010_survey_of_lawyers_funds_for_client_protection.authcheckdam.pdf.
27. *Id.*
28. *Id.*
29. LAWYER REGULATION FOR A NEW CENTURY: REPORT OF THE COMMISSION ON EVALUATION OF DISCIPLINARY ENFORCEMENT 76 (ABA 1992), *available at* http://www.americanbar.org/groups/professional_responsibility/resources/report_archive/mckay_report.html.
30. *Id.* at 76–78.

Appendix A

NALA Code of Ethics and Professional Responsibility

▶ PREAMBLE

A paralegal must adhere strictly to the accepted standards of legal ethics and to the general principles of proper conduct. The performance of the duties of the paralegal shall be governed by specific canons as defined herein so that justice will be served and goals of the profession attained. (*See* NALA Model Standards and Guidelines for Utilization of Legal Assistants, Section II.)

The canons of ethics set forth hereafter are adopted by the National Association of Legal Assistants, Inc., as a general guide intended to aid paralegals and attorneys. The enumeration of these rules does not mean there are not others of equal importance although not specifically mentioned. Court rules, agency rules, and statutes must be taken into consideration when interpreting the canons.

Reprinted with permission of the National Association of Legal Assistants, Inc. Inquiries should be directed to NALA, 1516 S. Boston, Suite 200, Tulsa, OK 74119, or by e-mail to nalanet@nala.org.

Definition

Legal assistants, also known as paralegals, are a distinguishable group of persons who assist attorneys in the delivery of legal services. Through formal education, training, and experience, legal assistants have knowledge and expertise regarding the legal system and substantive and procedural law which qualify them to do work of a legal nature under the supervision of an attorney.

In 2001, NALA members also adopted the ABA definition of a legal assistant/paralegal, as follows:

> A legal assistant or paralegal is a person qualified by education, training or work experience who is employed or retained by a lawyer, law office, corporation, governmental agency or other entity who performs specifically delegated substantive legal work for which a lawyer is responsible. (Adopted by the ABA in 1997)

Canon 1—A paralegal must not perform any of the duties that attorneys only may perform nor take any actions that attorneys may not take.

Canon 2—A paralegal may perform any task which is properly delegated and supervised by an attorney, as long as the attorney is ultimately responsible to the client, maintains a direct relationship with the client, and assumes professional responsibility for the work product.

Canon 3—A paralegal must not:

    a. engage in, encourage, or contribute to any act which could constitute the unauthorized practice of law; and

    b. establish attorney-client relationships, set fees, give legal opinions or advice, or represent a client before a court or agency unless so authorized by that court or agency; and

    c. engage in conduct or take any action which would assist or involve the attorney in a violation of professional ethics or give the appearance of professional impropriety.

Canon 4—A paralegal must use discretion and professional judgment commensurate with knowledge and experience but must not render independent legal judgment in place of an attorney. The services of an attorney are essential in the public interest whenever such legal judgment is required.

Canon 5—A paralegal must disclose his or her status as a paralegal at the outset of any professional relationship with a client, attorney, a court or administrative agency or personnel thereof, or a member of the general public. A paralegal must act prudently in determining the extent to which a client may be assisted without the presence of an attorney.

Canon 6—A paralegal must strive to maintain integrity and a high degree of competency through education and training with respect to professional responsibility, local rules and practice, and through continuing education in substantive areas of law to better assist the legal profession in fulfilling its duty to provide legal service.

Canon 7—A paralegal must protect the confidences of a client and must not violate any rule or statute now in effect or hereafter enacted controlling the doctrine of privileged communications between a client and an attorney.

Canon 8—A paralegal must disclose to his or her employer or prospective employer any pre-existing client or personal relationship that may conflict with the interests of the employer or prospective employer and/or their clients.

Canon 9—A paralegal must do all other things incidental, necessary, or expedient for the attainment of the ethics and responsibilities as defined by statute or rule of court.

Canon 10—A paralegal's conduct is guided by bar associations' codes of professional responsibility and rules of professional conduct.

Appendix B

NFPA Model Code of Ethics and Professional Responsibility and Guidelines for Enforcement

PREAMBLE

The National Federation of Paralegal Associations, Inc. [NFPA] is a professional organization comprised of paralegal associations and individual paralegals throughout the United States and Canada. Members of NFPA have varying backgrounds, experiences, education, and job responsibilities that reflect the diversity of the paralegal profession. NFPA promotes the growth, development, and recognition of the paralegal profession as an integral partner in the delivery of legal services.

In May 1993 NFPA adopted its Model Code of Ethics and Professional Responsibility ("Model Code") to delineate the principles for ethics and conduct to which every paralegal should aspire.

Many paralegal associations throughout the United States have endorsed the concept and content of NFPA's Model

---

Reprinted by permission from the National Federation of Paralegal Associations, Inc., www.paralegals.org.

Code through the adoption of their own ethical codes. In doing so, paralegals have confirmed the profession's commitment to increase the quality and efficiency of legal services, as well as recognized its responsibilities to the public, the legal community, and colleagues.

Paralegals have recognized, and will continue to recognize, that the profession must continue to evolve to enhance their roles in the delivery of legal services. With increased levels of responsibility comes the need to define and enforce mandatory rules of professional conduct. Enforcement of codes of paralegal conduct is a logical and necessary step to enhance and ensure the confidence of the legal community and the public in the integrity and professional responsibility of paralegals.

In April 1997 NFPA adopted the Model Disciplinary Rules ("Model Rules") to make possible the enforcement of the Canons and Ethical Considerations contained in the NFPA Model Code. A concurrent determination was made that the Model Code of Ethics and Professional Responsibility, formerly aspirational in nature, should be recognized as setting forth the enforceable obligations of all paralegals.

The Model Code and Model Rules offer a framework for professional discipline, either voluntarily or through formal regulatory programs.

§1. NFPA Model Disciplinary Rules and Ethical Considerations

1.1 A PARALEGAL SHALL ACHIEVE AND MAINTAIN A HIGH LEVEL OF COMPETENCE.

Ethical Considerations

EC-1.1(a) A paralegal shall aspire to participate in a minimum of twelve (12) hours of continuing legal education, to include at least one (1) hour of ethics education, every two (2) years in order to remain current on developments in the law.

EC-1.1(b) A paralegal shall participate in continuing education in order to keep informed of current legal, technical, and general developments.

EC-1.1(c) A paralegal shall perform all assignments promptly and efficiently.

1.2 A PARALEGAL SHALL MAINTAIN A HIGH LEVEL OF PERSONAL AND PROFESSIONAL INTEGRITY.

Ethical Considerations

EC-1.2(a) A paralegal shall not engage in any ex parte communications involving the courts or any other adjudicatory body in an attempt to exert undue influence or to obtain advantage or the benefit of only one party.

EC-1.2(b) A paralegal shall not communicate, or cause another to communicate, with a party the paralegal knows to be represented by a lawyer in a pending matter without the prior consent of the lawyer representing such other party.

EC-1.2(c) A paralegal shall ensure that all timekeeping and billing records prepared by the paralegal are thorough, accurate, honest, and complete.

EC-1.2(d) A paralegal shall not knowingly engage in fraudulent billing practices. Such practices may include, but are not limited to: inflation of hours billed to a client or employer; misrepresentation of the nature of tasks performed; and/or submission of fraudulent expense and disbursement documentation.

EC-1.2(e) A paralegal shall be scrupulous, thorough, and honest in the identification and maintenance of all funds, securities, and other assets of a client and shall provide accurate accounting as appropriate.

EC-1.2(f) A paralegal shall advise the proper authority of non-confidential knowledge of any dishonest or fraudulent acts by any person pertaining to the handling of the funds, securities, or other assets of a client. The authority to whom the report is made shall depend on the nature and circumstances of the possible misconduct (e.g., ethics committees of law firms, corporations and/or paralegal associations, local or state bar associations, local prosecutors, administrative agencies, etc.). Failure to report such knowledge is in itself misconduct and shall be treated as such under these rules.

1.3 A PARALEGAL SHALL MAINTAIN A HIGH STANDARD OF PROFESSIONAL CONDUCT.

Ethical Considerations

EC-1.3(a) A paralegal shall refrain from engaging in any conduct that offends the dignity and decorum of proceedings before a court or other adjudicatory body and shall be respectful of all rules and procedures.

EC-1.3(b) A paralegal shall avoid impropriety and the appearance of impropriety and shall not engage in any conduct that would adversely affect his/her fitness to practice. Such conduct may include, but is not limited to: violence, dishonesty, interference with the administration of justice, and/or abuse of a professional position or public office.

EC-1.3(c) Should a paralegal's fitness to practice be compromised by physical or mental illness, causing that paralegal to commit an act that is in direct violation of the Model Code/Model Rules and/or the rules and/or laws governing the jurisdiction in which the paralegal practices, that paralegal may be protected from sanction upon review of the nature and circumstances of that illness.

EC-1.3(d) A paralegal shall advise the proper authority of non-confidential knowledge of any action of another legal professional that clearly demonstrates fraud, deceit, dishonesty, or misrepresentation. The authority to whom the report is made shall depend on the nature and circumstances of the possible misconduct (e.g., ethics committees of law firms, corporations and/or paralegal associations, local or state bar associations, local prosecutors, administrative agencies, etc.). Failure to report such knowledge is in itself misconduct and shall be treated as such under these rules.

EC-1.3(e) A paralegal shall not knowingly assist any individual with the commission of an act that is in direct violation of the Model Code/Model Rules and/or the rules and/or laws governing the jurisdiction in which the paralegal practices.

EC-1.3(f) If a paralegal possesses knowledge of future criminal activity, that knowledge must be reported to the appropriate authority immediately.

1.4 A PARALEGAL SHALL SERVE THE PUBLIC INTEREST BY CONTRIBUTING TO THE DELIVERY OF QUALITY LEGAL SERVICES AND THE IMPROVEMENT OF THE LEGAL SYSTEM.

Ethical Considerations

EC-1.4(a) A paralegal shall be sensitive to the legal needs of the public and shall promote the development and implementation of programs that address those needs.

EC-1.4(b) A paralegal shall support efforts to improve the legal system and access thereto and shall assist in making changes.

EC-1.4(c) A paralegal shall support and participate in the delivery of Pro Bono Publico services directed toward implementing and improving access to justice, the law, the legal system, or the paralegal and legal professions.

EC-1.4(d) A paralegal should aspire annually to contribute twenty-four (24) hours of Pro Bono Publico services under the supervision of an attorney or as authorized by administrative, statutory, or court authority to:

   1. *persons of limited means; or*

   2. *charitable, religious, civic, community, governmental, and educational organizations in matters that are designed primarily to address the legal needs of persons with limited means; or*

   3. *individuals, groups, or organizations seeking to secure or protect civil rights, civil liberties, or public rights.*

1.5 A PARALEGAL SHALL PRESERVE ALL CONFIDENTIAL INFORMATION PROVIDED BY THE CLIENT OR ACQUIRED FROM OTHER SOURCES BEFORE, DURING, AND AFTER THE COURSE OF THE PROFESSIONAL RELATIONSHIP.

Ethical Considerations

EC-1.5(a) A paralegal shall be aware of and abide by all legal authority governing confidential information in the jurisdiction in which the paralegal practices.

EC-1.5(b) A paralegal shall not use confidential information to the disadvantage of the client.

EC-1.5(c) A paralegal shall not use confidential information to the advantage of the paralegal or of a third person.

EC-1.5(d) A paralegal may reveal confidential information only after full disclosure and with the client's written consent; or, when required by law or court order; or, when necessary to prevent the client from committing an act that could result in death or serious bodily harm.

EC-1.5(e) A paralegal shall keep those individuals responsible for the legal representation of a client fully informed of any confidential information the paralegal may have pertaining to that client.

EC-1.5(f) A paralegal shall not engage in any indiscreet communications concerning clients.

1.6 A PARALEGAL SHALL AVOID CONFLICTS OF INTEREST AND SHALL DISCLOSE ANY POSSIBLE CONFLICT TO THE EMPLOYER OR CLIENT, AS WELL AS TO THE PROSPECTIVE EMPLOYERS OR CLIENTS.

Ethical Considerations

EC-1.6(a) A paralegal shall act within the bounds of the law, solely for the benefit of the client, and shall be free of compromising influences and loyalties. Neither the paralegal's personal or business interest, nor those of other clients or third persons, should compromise the paralegal's professional judgment and loyalty to the client.

EC-1.6(b) A paralegal shall avoid conflicts of interest that may arise from previous assignments, whether for a present or past employer or client.

EC-1.6(c) A paralegal shall avoid conflicts of interest that may arise from family relationships and from personal and business interests.

EC-1.6(d) In order to be able to determine whether an actual or potential conflict of interest exists a paralegal shall create and maintain an effective recordkeeping system that identifies clients, matters, and parties with which the paralegal has worked.

EC-1.6(e) A paralegal shall reveal sufficient non-confidential information about a client or former client to reasonably ascertain if an actual or potential conflict of interest exists.

EC-1.6(f) A paralegal shall not participate in or conduct work on any matter where a conflict of interest has been identified.

EC-1.6(g) In matters where a conflict of interest has been identified and the client consents to continued representation, a paralegal shall comply fully with the implementation and maintenance of an Ethical Wall.

1.7 A PARALEGAL'S TITLE SHALL BE FULLY DISCLOSED.

Ethical Considerations

EC-1.7(a) A paralegal's title shall clearly indicate the individual's status and shall be disclosed in all business and professional communications to avoid misunderstandings and misconceptions about the paralegal's role and responsibilities.

EC-1.7(b) A paralegal's title shall be included if the paralegal's name appears on business cards, letterhead, brochures, directories, and advertisements.

EC-1.7(c) A paralegal shall not use letterhead, business cards, or other promotional materials to create a fraudulent impression of his/her status or ability to practice in the jurisdiction in which the paralegal practices.

EC-1.7(d) A paralegal shall not practice under color of any record, diploma, or certificate that has been illegally or fraudulently obtained or issued or which is misrepresentative in any way.

EC-1.7(e) A paralegal shall not participate in the creation, issuance, or dissemination of fraudulent records, diplomas, or certificates.

1.8 A PARALEGAL SHALL NOT ENGAGE IN THE UNAUTHORIZED PRACTICE OF LAW.

Ethical Considerations

EC-1.8(a) A paralegal shall comply with the applicable legal authority governing the unauthorized practice of law in the jurisdiction in which the paralegal practices.

Appendix C

ABA Model Guidelines for the Utilization of Paralegal Services

Guideline 1: A lawyer is responsible for all of the professional actions of a paralegal performing services at the lawyer's direction and should take reasonable measures to ensure that the paralegal's conduct is consistent with the lawyer's obligations under the rules of professional conduct of the jurisdiction in which the lawyer practices.

Guideline 2: Provided the lawyer maintains responsibility for the work product, a lawyer may delegate to a paralegal any task normally performed by the lawyer except those tasks proscribed to a nonlawyer by statute, court rule, administrative rule or regulation, controlling authority, the applicable rule of professional conduct of the jurisdiction in which the lawyer practices, or these Guidelines.

Copyright ©2012 American Bar Association. All rights reserved.

Guideline 3: A lawyer may not delegate to a paralegal:

(a) Responsibility for establishing an attorney-client relationship.

(b) Responsibility for establishing the amount of a fee to be charged for a legal service.

(c) Responsibility for a legal opinion rendered to a client.

Guideline 4: A lawyer is responsible for taking reasonable measures to ensure that clients, courts, and other lawyers are aware that a paralegal, whose services are utilized by the lawyer in performing legal services, is not licensed to practice law.

Guideline 5: A lawyer may identify paralegals by name and title on the lawyer's letterhead and on business cards identifying the lawyer's firm.

Guideline 6: A lawyer is responsible for taking reasonable measures to ensure that all client confidences are preserved by a paralegal.

Guideline 7: A lawyer should take reasonable measures to prevent conflicts of interest resulting from a paralegal's other employment or interests.

Guideline 8: A lawyer may include a charge for the work performed by a paralegal in setting a charge and/or billing for legal services.

Guideline 9: A lawyer may not split legal fees with a paralegal nor pay a paralegal for the referral of legal business. A lawyer may compensate a paralegal based on the quantity and quality of the paralegal's work and the value of that work to a law practice, but the paralegal's compensation may not be contingent, by advance agreement, upon the outcome of a particular case or class of cases.

Guideline 10: A lawyer who employs a paralegal should facilitate the paralegal's participation in appropriate continuing education and pro bono publico activities.

Appendix D

AAfPE Core Competencies for Paralegal Programs (October 2013)

◆ CRITICAL THINKING SKILLS

Paralegal education programs should be able to demonstrate that their graduates can:

__1.__   Analyze a problem and identify issues relevant to a potential solution;

__2.__   Determine which areas of law are relevant to a particular situation;

__3.__   Identify interrelationships among cases, statutes, regulations, and other legal authorities;

__4.__   Synthesize and apply recognized legal authority to the solution of a problem;

__5.__   Formulate logical solutions to problems; construct logical arguments in support of specific positions; evaluate solutions and arguments;

Reprinted with permission.

6. Identify and evaluate alternative solutions;
7. Apply principles of professional ethics to specific factual situations;
8. Analyze factual situations to determine when it is appropriate to apply exceptions to general legal rules;
9. Apply exceptions to general legal rules;
10. Distinguish evidentiary facts from other material and/or controlling facts;
11. Identify factual omissions and inconsistencies; and
12. Discern and analyze the law applicable to all parties to a dispute.

♦ ORGANIZATIONAL SKILLS

Paralegal education programs should be able to demonstrate that their graduates can:

1. Sort information by category;
2. Prioritize assignments and client needs;
3. Manage information and client files manually and electronically;
4. Understand and use manual and electronic calendaring systems;
5. Understand and utilize e-filing systems;
6. Understand the ethical guidelines associated with file and client information maintenance;
7. When appropriate, manage social media on behalf of an employer;
8. Provide appropriate hearing/trial assistance through the organization and maintenance of evidence;
9. Create materials that show organizational skills like trial notebooks; and
10. Utilize time efficiently.

◆ GENERAL COMMUNICATION SKILLS

Paralegal education programs should be able to demonstrate that their graduates can:

1. Interact effectively, in person, by telephone, in written and electronic correspondence with lawyers, clients, witnesses, court personnel, co-workers, and other business professionals;
2. Conduct effective interviews with clients, witnesses, and experts;
3. Exhibit tact and diplomacy; distinguish between assertive and aggressive behavior; apply assertive behavior techniques;
4. Adapt to situations as they arise;
5. Multi-task;
6. Understand the need to ask questions and seek guidance when appropriate;
7. Identify attributes of a team player; work effectively as part of a team;
8. Work independently and with a minimal amount of supervision when appropriate; and
9. Understand the boundaries, limitations and prohibitions related to communications with opposing counsel, opposing parties, and court personnel.

◆ LEGAL RESEARCH SKILLS

Legal research involves the application of the critical thinking, organizational, and communication skills listed above. Paralegal education programs should be able to demonstrate that their graduates can:

1. Prepare and carry out a legal research plan; analyze and categorize key facts as well as relevant missing facts in a situation;
2. Use both print and electronic sources of law to locate applicable statutes, administrative regulations, constitutional provisions, court cases, and other primary source materials;

___3.___ Understand which sources of law supersede other sources of law;

___4.___ Use both print and electronic sources of law to locate treatises, law review articles, legal encyclopedias, and other secondary source materials that help explain the law;

___5.___ Read, evaluate, and analyze both print and electronic sources of law, and apply them to issues requiring legal analysis;

___6.___ Properly cite both print and electronic sources of law;

___7.___ "Cite check" legal sources;

___8.___ Identify, locate, and appropriately use both print and electronic resources to update and verify the reliability of cited legal authority;

___9.___ Understand whether your jurisdiction accepts or permits the use of unpublished/depublished opinions in legal documents; and

___10.___ Properly locate and identify binding and persuasive authority.

♦ LEGAL WRITING SKILLS

Legal writing involves the application of the critical thinking, organizational, communications, and legal research skills listed above. Paralegal education programs should be able to demonstrate that their graduates can:

___1.___ Understand and apply principles of writing and rules of English grammar to all writing tasks;

___2.___ Write in a style that conveys legal theory in a clear and concise manner;

___3.___ Read and apply a court opinion to a fact situation;

___4.___ Report legal research findings in a standard interoffice memorandum or other appropriate format;

___5.___ Cite print and electronic primary and secondary sources in proper form;

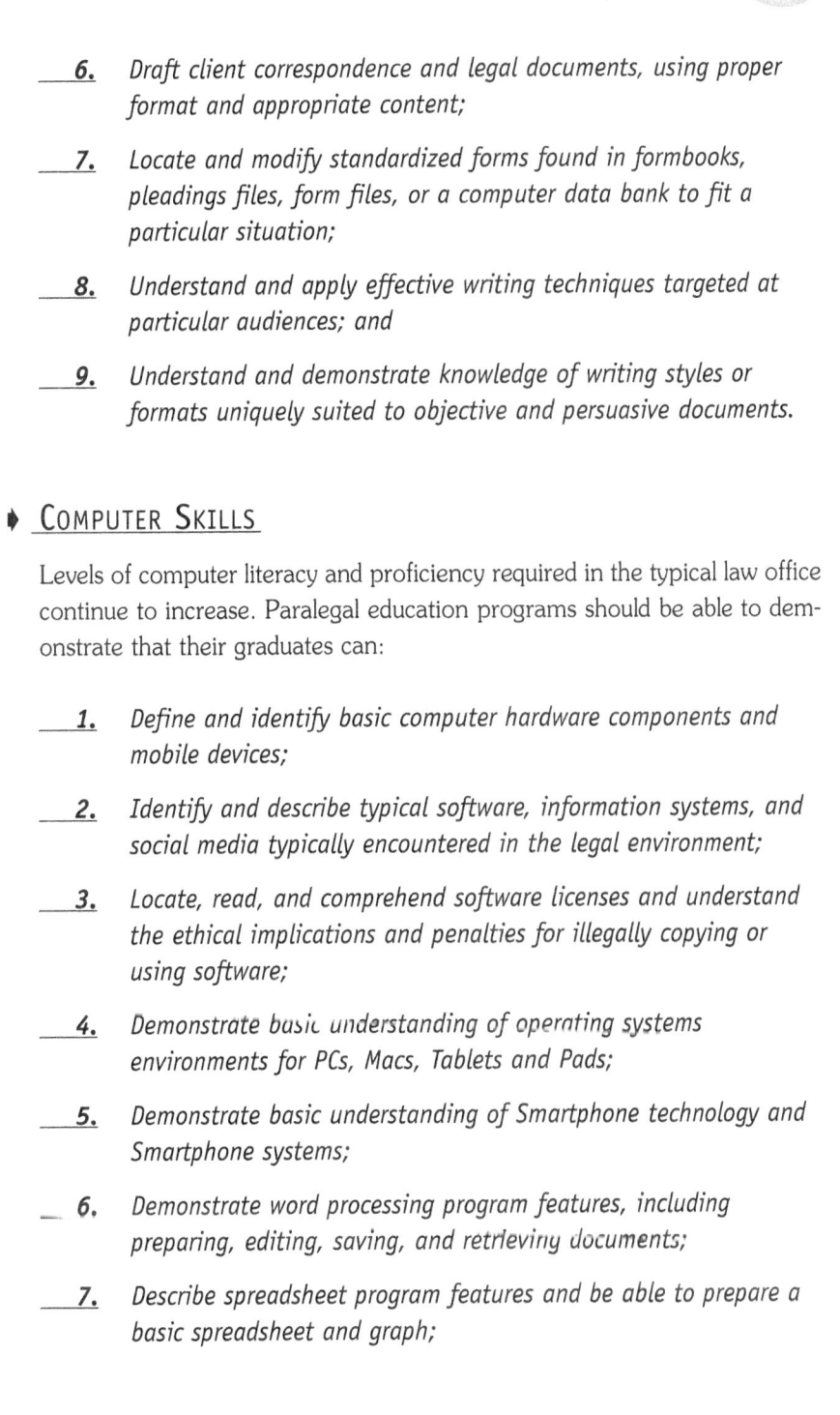

___6.___ Draft client correspondence and legal documents, using proper format and appropriate content;

___7.___ Locate and modify standardized forms found in formbooks, pleadings files, form files, or a computer data bank to fit a particular situation;

___8.___ Understand and apply effective writing techniques targeted at particular audiences; and

___9.___ Understand and demonstrate knowledge of writing styles or formats uniquely suited to objective and persuasive documents.

♦ COMPUTER SKILLS

Levels of computer literacy and proficiency required in the typical law office continue to increase. Paralegal education programs should be able to demonstrate that their graduates can:

___1.___ Define and identify basic computer hardware components and mobile devices;

___2.___ Identify and describe typical software, information systems, and social media typically encountered in the legal environment;

___3.___ Locate, read, and comprehend software licenses and understand the ethical implications and penalties for illegally copying or using software;

___4.___ Demonstrate basic understanding of operating systems environments for PCs, Macs, Tablets and Pads;

___5.___ Demonstrate basic understanding of Smartphone technology and Smartphone systems;

___6.___ Demonstrate word processing program features, including preparing, editing, saving, and retrieving documents;

___7.___ Describe spreadsheet program features and be able to prepare a basic spreadsheet and graph;

___8.___   Describe database program features and be able to prepare a basic database;

___9.___   Describe the features of a presentation software program including slide components, graphics, and sound and be able to prepare a basic presentation;

___10.___ Describe features of typical law office time keeping and billing software programs; identify ethical issues that arise with the use of such programs;

___11.___ Describe the features of computerized litigation support programs and be able to compare such programs to corresponding manual litigation support;

___12.___ Describe the features of case management and information management software; compare to corresponding manual case management;

___13.___ Describe the features of computerized docket control systems; compare to corresponding manual docket control systems; identify ethical problems relating to docket control;

___14.___ Access legal and non-legal data available on the Internet; compare key word and subject-oriented search engines; evaluate Internet sites for reliability and validity of information; locate and join sites that relate to the legal assistant career;

___15.___ Use e-mail functions and social media; describe ethical issues that arise as a result of using e-mail and other electronic methods of communication including cloud computing;

___16.___ Describe the process used to file electronically documents in courts that permit electronic filing; compare to manual filing; identify ethical problems related to electronic filing of court documents;

___17.___ Perform computer assisted legal research and Internet legal and factual research; and

___18.___ Identify factors and issues to consider when purchasing legal-specific software.

Appendix D

♦ INTERVIEWING AND INVESTIGATION SKILLS

Interviewing and investigation involves the application of critical thinking, organizational, communication, research, writing, and computer skills listed above. Paralegal education programs should be able to demonstrate that their graduates can:

   1. Identify and locate witnesses, potential parties to a suit, and experts;

   2. Develop a list of questions for an interview; conduct an effective interview; record the interview accurately;

   3. Locate and prepare request documents to obtain information that is commonly maintained by government entities; obtain such information; read and interpret the information contained in such records and apply to a given situation;

   4. Prepare releases and requests to obtain medical, corporate and other non-governmental records; obtain such records; read and interpret the information contained in such records and apply to a given situation;

   5. Locate and apply rules of evidence and procedure to document acquisition, and witness, parties and expert testimony derived from interviews; and

   6. Perform Internet searches to obtain relevant and reliable information.

♦ THE PARALEGAL PROFESSION AND ETHICAL OBLIGATIONS

Knowledge and information relating to the role of the paralegal in the delivery of legal services, ethics, and professional values is vital to paralegal competence. Paralegal education programs should be able to demonstrate that their graduates can:

   1. Understand the legal process and the nature of law practice, emphasizing the role of the paralegal in the delivery of legal services;

2. Understand the ways in which paralegal services are used in the delivery of legal services, including functions and tasks commonly performed by paralegals; the place of the paralegal in the delivery services team; the respective roles and responsibilities of the members of the legal team;

3. Understand the evolving role of the paralegal and other non-lawyers in the delivery of legal services and in increasing access to legal services;

4. Identify the professional associations that serve and promote the paralegal profession; understand the importance of participation in professional activities;

5. Understand the legal and ethical principles that guide paralegal conduct, including, but not limited to: unauthorized practice of law and lawyer supervision of non-lawyers; confidentiality and attorney-client privilege; conflicts of interest; competence; advertising and solicitation; handling client funds, legal fees, and related matters such as attorney fee awards and fee agreements; prohibitions relating to fees including fee referrals, fee-splitting, and partnerships between lawyers and non-lawyers; limitations on communications with persons outside law firms, including represented persons, judges, jurors; special rules relating to litigation such as proper courtroom conduct, honesty and candor, frivolous claims and defenses, sanctions for misconduct;

6. Demonstrate the ability to identify and resolve ethical dilemmas that may be confronted in the workplace; and

7. Understand the importance of continuing legal education for paralegals.

♦ Law Office Management Skills

Basic knowledge of the fundamentals of law office management and organization is essential to the entry-level paralegal. This knowledge can be presented through a stand-alone course or as part of the general program curriculum. Paralegal education programs should be able to demonstrate that their graduates can:

1. Identify and explain basic principles of management;
2. Explain issues relating to employment and promotion of paralegals;
3. Identify and describe the different types of law offices including organization, management, and personnel structure;
4. Identify and explain the different management, administrative, and support roles performed by lawyers and non-lawyers in the law office;
5. Describe law office billing practices, accounting systems, and methods used for determining cost of legal services;
6. Understand administrative systems used in law practice, including client relation systems, conflict management, personnel, docket/calendaring systems, billing systems, and risk management systems;
7. Explain the role of technology in the management and administration of the law office; and
8. Identify and explain acceptable marketing and advertising practices for promoting law firms and legal services.

Appendix E

Legal Research Resources

Paralegals often perform legal research, including legal ethics research. In order to research an ethics inquiry effectively, a paralegal must become familiar with the basic texts and materials in the field. This appendix offers a method for categorizing most legal ethics materials and then lists some of the most useful tools for answering ethics questions.

◆ RESEARCH SOURCES AND TOOLS

Most of the materials available in a law library can be loosely organized into four main categories: primary sources, secondary sources, finding tools, and updating tools. Some research sources, such as the legal databases on a computer, contain all four categories. Whether one is researching in the substantive areas of torts, contracts, or legal ethics, different kinds of sources are needed for various stages of legal research. Generally, primary and secondary sources contain substantive information that is located and updated through finding and updating tools.

♦ WEIGHT OF AUTHORITY

An important concept in legal research is the weight of legal authority. In order to conduct competent research, the researcher must be able to analyze the relative importance of the cases, books, or documents being reviewed.

One helpful way to sift through all the available material is to distinguish between "mandatory authority"—those sources that a court in a particular jurisdiction must consider—and "persuasive authority"—other sources that a court may or may not find useful in reaching a decision. Courts are bound by mandatory authority; they must follow the rules, statutes, and cases in their own jurisdiction and those of any higher power, such as an appellate court. Persuasive authority is all other types of information that might "persuade" a court to rule in a certain way. Thus, relevant cases from neighboring jurisdictions, treatises, scholarly articles, or books might be cited as persuasive authority. A court may ignore such sources or rely upon them in the formulation of a decision, especially in a novel area of law.

♦ RESEARCH AND TECHNOLOGY

In addition to being familiar with traditional library research materials, a paralegal should be aware of other technology-based resources that can improve productivity. For example, Wolters Kluwer offers ebooks to aid in tax research.

The most commonly used online services are LexisNexis, Westlaw, and Bloomberg Law. Because these services come with a fee, the paralegal should be aware of firm policy regarding time spent using them in general and for any particular client. There are also many free online legal information sites, such as Google Scholar. Courts and branches of state and federal government often have sites that provide opinions, statutes, and rules. These are official sources of information. However, there are many other sites where the source or accuracy of the information is unclear. Thus, the paralegal should be very careful in relying upon the information provided at such sites.

The Internet has become a valuable tool for ethics research. There are an increasing number of websites dealing with lawyer ethics, including state bar association sites that publish ethics opinions. The ABA Center for Professional Responsibility maintains a links page that connects to the rules of professional conduct in every jurisdiction and the ethics opinions of most.[1]

Though the Internet can provide quick and easy access to a variety of information, a paralegal should be careful about citing to Internet sources. The 19th edition of *The Bluebook: A Uniform System of Citation* provides a method of citation to Internet sources but states that "[a]n Internet source may be cited directly when it does not exist in a traditional printed format or when a traditional printed source, such as a letter or unpublished dissertation, exists but cannot be found or is so obscure that it is practically unavailable."[2]

♦ ETHICS RESEARCH SERVICES

In addition to the above-mentioned materials, services, and products, the paralegal should be aware that a number of bar associations operate ethics research services. For example, the ABA Center for Professional Responsibility operates ETHIC Search for those needing information on ABA rules, standards, and ethics opinions.[3]

Outdated law can be worse than no law at all. It can be embarrassing, damaging, and a violation of a jurisdiction's rules of professional conduct to cite a statute or case that has been overturned or to fail to cite an opposing authority. To avoid this hazard, a legal researcher must use special updating services, such as WestCheck, to ensure that the law the researcher relies upon is currently valid.

Websites for Legal Ethics Research

ABA Center for Professional Responsibility
Links to state rules of professional conduct, state (and some local) ethics opinions, state codes of judicial conduct.

    http://www.americanbar.org/groups/professional_responsibility.html

    http://ambar.org/CPRHome

    http://www.americanbar.org/groups/professional_responsibility/resources/links_of_interest.html

Freivogel on Conflicts
A practical online guide to conflicts of interest for lawyers with sophisticated business and litigation practices.
   http://www.freivogelonconflicts.com/

Bloomberg Law
   http://about.bloomberglaw.com/

Google Scholar
   http://scholar.google.com/

LexisNexis
   http://www.lexisnexis.com/

Westlaw
   http://web2.westlaw.com/signon/default.wl?newdoor=true&rs=home1%2E0&vr=2%2E0

Relative Weight of Legal Authority

Persuasive Authority	Mandatory Authority
▸ ABA ethics opinions	▸ U.S. Constitution
▸ model guidelines	▸ U.S. Supreme Court decisions
▸ model rules	▸ U.S. Court of Appeals decisions
▸ cases from neighboring jurisdictions; including appellate decisions from different circuits in same state	▸ U.S. District Court decisions
	▸ federal and state statutes
	▸ rules of professional conduct promulgated by the highest court in a jurisdiction
▸ statutes from neighboring jurisdictions	▸ decisions from the highest court in a jurisdiction
▸ state and local bar ethics opinions	▸ decisions from appellate court in a jurisdiction
▸ law review articles	
▸ treatises	
▸ decisions by lawyer disciplinary authorities	

Appendix E 173

A Key to the Law Library

PRIMARY AUTHORITY

LOCATING TOOLS   UPDATING TOOLS

SECONDARY AUTHORITY

Sources

The substantive materials in the law library fall into two categories: primary authority and secondary authority. Primary authority includes judicial opinions, statutes, rules, and regulations. Secondary authority explains, criticizes, or otherwise discusses the law. Examples of secondary authorities are law review articles and hornbooks.

Tools

The law library has two types of tools especially designed for legal research: locating tools and updating tools. Locating tools help the researcher to find the primary and secondary authorities. Examples of locating tools are digests of cases and indexes to statutes. Updating tools help to gauge the current validity of the law. Examples of updating tools are citators and a pocket part to a state statute book containing the current law.

Research Tip

Updating tools can also serve as locating tools on occasion: if a researcher has a particular case in mind, an updating tool, such as a citator, will list other cases discussing the cited case.

Sometimes a primary authority will cite secondary authorities providing another helpful means of finding source material.

What's What in Ethics Research

Publication	Contents	Functions
ABA Model Rules of Professional Conduct	1983 national model of professional standards governing the practice of law. Some form of these rules has been adopted in most jurisdictions.	Secondary Source
ABA Model Code of Judicial Conduct	2007 national model for judicial ethics.	Secondary Source
ABA Ethics Opinions	ABA Formal Opinions 84-349 through 98-412.	Secondary Source
Formal Ethics Opinions, 1999–2013	ABA Formal Ethics Opinions 99-413 through -462	Secondary Source
Formal and Informal Ethics Opinions 1983–1998	Contains ABA Formal Opinions 84-349 through 98-412, issued from 1984 to 1998; contains Informal Opinions 83-1496 through 89-1530, issued from 1983 to 1989 (the ABA stopped issuing informal opinions after 1989). These opinions interpret the Model Rules of Professional Conduct.	Secondary Source
Annotated Model Rules of Professional Conduct	Model Rules and legal background notes analyzing cases, opinions, law review articles, and legal treatises.	Secondary Source Locating Tool

Publication	Contents	Functions
Annotated Model Code of Judicial Conduct	Model Code and legal background notes analyzing cases, opinions, law review articles, and legal treatises.	Secondary Source Locating Tool
Annotated Standards for Imposing Lawyer Sanctions	Model Standards and legal background notes analyzing cases, opinions, law review articles, and legal treatises.	Secondary Source Locating Tool
A Legislative History: The Development of the ABA Model Rules of Professional Conduct, 1982–2013	Traces the development of the Model Rules in the House of Delegates, including amendments made and arguments advanced in support of and in opposition to those amendments.	Secondary Source
Shepard's Professional and Judicial Conduct Citations	A citator with quarterly listings of cases, rules, and opinions on ethics.	Updating Tool Locating Source
Charles Gardner Geyh and W. William Hodes, *Reporters' Notes to the Model Code of Judicial Conduct*	Model Code of Judicial Conduct, historical notes, and comment.	Secondary Source Locating Tool
Geoffrey C. Hazard, W. William Hodes, and Peter R. Jarvis, *The Law of Lawyering*	A legal treatise on the law of professional responsibility.	Secondary Source Locating Tool

Publication	Contents	Functions
ABA/BNA Lawyers' Manual on Professional Conduct	A nationally recognized legal notification service: the manual is a source for all subjects that come under the umbrella topic of professional conduct; the Current Reports offers biweekly information and analysis on recent ethics opinions, disciplinary proceedings, and court decisions in the area of professional conduct; and the ethics opinions compose the only national collection of digests of state and local bar association ethics committee opinions that interpret the rules of the jurisdiction issuing the opinion.	Secondary Source Locating Tool Updating Tool
Thomas D. Morgan	A comparison of the ABA Model Rules of Professional Conduct and the ALI Restatement (Third) of the Law Governing Lawyers.	Secondary Source Locating Tool
Charles W. Wolfram, Modern Legal Ethics	A legal treatise on the law of professional responsibility.	Secondary Source Locating Tool

Publication	Contents	Functions
Ronald D. Rotunda and John S. Dzienkowski, Legal Ethics: The Lawyer's Deskbook on Professional Responsibility	A legal treatise on the law of professional responsibility.	Secondary Source Locating Tool
ABA Compendium of Professional Responsibility Rules and Standards	A compilation of ABA Model Rules and Standards for ethical and professional conduct, various related federal rules, and key ABA ethics opinions.	Primary Source Secondary Source
Stephen Gillers, Roy D. Simon, Andrew M. Perlman, and John Steele Regulation of Lawyers: Statutes and Standards	A compendium of rules regulating the conduct of lawyers and judges.	Secondary Source Locating Tool
ALI [American Law Institute] Restatement of the Law Governing Lawyers	Consists of suggested rules of professional conduct followed by explanatory comments.	Secondary Source Locating Tool

◆ Notes

1. *See Links of Interest*, ABA, http://www.americanbar.org/groups/professional_responsibility/resources/links_of_interest.html (last visited Apr. 13. 2015).

2. THE BLUEBOOK: A UNIFORM SYSTEM OF CITATION R. 18.2.1, at 165 (Columbia Law Review Ass'n et al. eds., 19th ed. 2010).

3. *See ETHICSearch, ABA,* http://ambar.org/CPREthicsearch (last visited Apr. 13, 2015). The Center for Professional Responsibility also provides links to some state ethics hotlines. *See Links of Interest, supra* note 1.

Appendix F

Model Rules for Client Trust Account Records (Adopted August 2010)

RULE 1: RECORDKEEPING GENERALLY

A lawyer who practices in this jurisdiction shall maintain current financial records as provided in these Rules and required by [Rule 1.15 of the Model Rules of Professional Conduct], and shall retain the following records for a period of [five years] after termination of the representation:

(a) receipt and disbursement journals containing a record of deposits to and withdrawals from client trust accounts, specifically identifying the date, source, and description of each item deposited, as well as the date, payee, and purpose of each disbursement;

(b) ledger records for all client trust accounts showing, for each separate trust client or beneficiary, the source of all funds deposited, the names of all persons for whom the funds are or were held, the amount of such funds, the descriptions and amounts of charges or withdrawals, and the names of all persons or entities to whom such funds were disbursed;

(c) copies of retainer and compensation agreements with clients [as required by Rule 1.5 of the Model Rules of Professional Conduct];

(d) copies of accountings to clients or third persons showing the disbursement of funds to them or on their behalf;

(e) copies of bills for legal fees and expenses rendered to clients;

(f) copies of records showing disbursements on behalf of clients;

(g) the physical or electronic equivalents of all checkbook registers, bank statements, records of deposit, pre-numbered canceled checks, and substitute checks provided by a financial institution;

(h) records of all electronic transfers from client trust accounts, including the name of the person authorizing transfer, the date of transfer, the name of the recipient, and confirmation from the financial institution of the trust account number from which money was withdrawn and the date and the time the transfer was completed;

(i) copies of [monthly] trial balances and [quarterly] reconciliations of the client trust accounts maintained by the lawyer; and

(j) copies of those portions of client files that are reasonably related to client trust account transactions.

Comment

[1] Rule 1 enumerates the basic financial records that a lawyer must maintain with regard to all trust accounts of a law firm. These include the standard books of account, and the supporting records that are necessary to safeguard and account for the receipt and disbursement of client or third person funds as required by Rule 1.15 of the Model Rules of Professional Conduct or its equivalent. Consistent with Rule 1.15, this Rule proposes that lawyers maintain client trust account records for a period of five years after termination of each particular legal engagement or representation. Although these Model Rules address the accepted use of a client trust account by a lawyer when holding client or third person funds, some jurisdictions may permit a lawyer to deposit certain advance fees for legal services into the lawyer's business or operating account. In those situations, the lawyer should still be guided by the standards contained in these Model Rules.

Appendix F

[2] Rule 1(g) requires that the physical or electronic equivalents of all checkbook registers, bank statements, records of deposit, pre-numbered canceled checks, and substitute checks be maintained for a period of five years after termination of each legal engagement or representation. The "Check Clearing for the 21st Century Act" or "Check 21 Act," codified at 12 U.S.C. § 5001 et. seq., recognizes "substitute checks" as the legal equivalent of an original check. A "substitute check" is defined at 12 U.S.C. § 5002(16) as a paper reproduction of the original check that contains an image of the front and back of the original check; bears a magnetic ink character recognition ("MICR") line containing all the information appearing on the MICR line of the original check; conforms with generally applicable industry standards for substitute checks; and is suitable for automated processing in the same manner as the original check. Banks, as defined in 12 U.S.C. § 5002(2), are not required to return to customers the original canceled checks. Most banks now provide electronic images of checks to customers who have access to their accounts on Internet-based websites. It is the lawyer's responsibility to download electronic images. Electronic images shall be maintained for the requisite number of years and shall be readily available for printing upon request or shall be printed and maintained for the requisite number of years.

[3] The ACH (Automated Clearing House) Network is an electronic funds transfer or payment system that primarily provides for the inter-bank clearing of electronic payments between originating and receiving participating financial institutions. ACH transactions are payment instructions to either debit or credit a deposit account. ACH payments are used in a variety of payment environments including bill payments, business-to-business payments, and government payments (e.g. tax refunds). In addition to the primary use of ACH transactions, retailers and third parties use the ACH system for other types of transactions including electronic check conversion (ECC). ECC is the process of transmitting MICR information from the bottom of a check, converting check payments to ACH transactions depending upon the authorization given by the account holder at the point-of-purchase. In this type of transaction, the lawyer should be careful to comply with the requirements of Rule 1(h).

[4] There are five types of check conversions where a lawyer should be careful to comply with the requirements of Rule 1(h). First, in a "point-of-purchase

conversion," a paper check is converted into a debit at the point of purchase and the paper check is returned to the issuer. Second, in a "back-office conversion," a paper check is presented at the point of purchase and is later converted into a debit and the paper check is destroyed. Third, in an "account-receivable conversion," a paper check is converted into a debit and the paper check is destroyed. Fourth, in a "telephone-initiated debit" or "check-by-phone" conversion, bank account information is provided via the telephone and the information is converted to a debit. Fifth, in a "web-initiated debit," an electronic payment is initiated through a secure web environment. Rule 1(h) applies to each of the type of electronic funds transfers described. All electronic funds transfers shall be recorded and a lawyer should not re-use a check number which has been previously used in an electronic transfer transaction.

[5] The potential of these records to serve as safeguards is realized only if the procedures set forth in Rule 1(i) are regularly performed. The trial balance is the sum of balances of each client's ledger card (or the electronic equivalent). Its value lies in comparing it on a monthly basis to a control balance. The control balance starts with the previous month's balance, then adds receipts from the Trust Receipts Journal and subtracts disbursements from the Trust Disbursements Journal. Once the total matches the trial balance, the reconciliation readily follows by adding amounts of any outstanding checks and subtracting any deposits not credited by the bank at month's end. This balance should agree with the bank statement. Quarterly reconciliation is recommended only as a minimum requirement; monthly reconciliation is the preferred practice given the difficulty of identifying an error (whether by the lawyer or the bank) among three months' transactions.

[6] In some situations, documentation in addition to that listed in paragraphs (a) through (i) of Rule 1 is necessary for a complete understanding of a trust account transaction. The type of document that a lawyer must retain under paragraph (j) because it is "reasonably related" to a client trust transaction will vary depending on the nature of the transaction and the significance of the document in shedding light on the transaction. Examples of documents that typically must be retained under this paragraph include correspondence between the client and lawyer relating to a disagreement over fees or costs or the distribution of proceeds, settlement agreements contemplating payment of funds, settlement statements issued to the client,

documentation relating to sharing litigation costs and attorney fees for subrogated claims, agreements for division of fees between lawyers, guarantees of payment to third parties out of proceeds recovered on behalf of a client, and copies of bills, receipts, or correspondence related to any payments to third parties on behalf of a client (whether made from the client's funds or from the lawyer's funds advanced for the benefit of the client).

RULE 2: CLIENT TRUST ACCOUNT SAFEGUARDS

With respect to client trust accounts required by [Rule 1.15 of the Model Rules of Professional Conduct]:

(a) only a lawyer admitted to practice law in this jurisdiction or a person under the direct supervision of the lawyer shall be an authorized signatory or authorize transfers from a client trust account;

(b) receipts shall be deposited intact and records of deposit should be sufficiently detailed to identify each item; and

(c) withdrawals shall be made only by check payable to a named payee and not to cash, or by authorized electronic transfer.

Comment

[1] Rule 2 enumerates minimal accounting controls for client trust accounts. It also enunciates the requirement that only a lawyer admitted to the practice of law in the jurisdiction or a person who is under the direct supervision of the lawyer shall be the authorized signatory or authorize electronic transfers from a client trust account. While it is permissible to grant limited nonlawyer access to a client trust account, such access should be limited and closely monitored by the lawyer. The lawyer has a non-delegable duty to protect and preserve the funds in a client trust account and can be disciplined for failure to supervise subordinates who misappropriate client funds. See, Rules 5.1 and 5.3 of the Model Rules of Professional Conduct.

[2] Authorized electronic transfers shall be limited to (1) money required for payment to a client or third person on behalf of a client; (2) expenses properly incurred on behalf of a client, such as filing fees or payment to third persons for services rendered in connection with the representation; or (3) money

transferred to the lawyer for fees that are earned in connection with the representation and are not in dispute; or (4) money transferred from one client trust account to another client trust account.

[3] The requirements in paragraph (b) that receipts shall be deposited intact mean that a lawyer cannot deposit one check or negotiable instrument into two or more accounts at the same time, a practice commonly known as a split deposit.

RULE 3: AVAILABILITY OF RECORDS

Records required by Rule 1 may be maintained by electronic, photographic, or other media provided that they otherwise comply with these Rules and that printed copies can be produced. These records shall be readily accessible to the lawyer.

Comment

[1] Rule 3 allows the use of alternative media for the maintenance of client trust account records if printed copies of necessary reports can be produced. If trust records are computerized, a system of regular and frequent (preferably daily) back-up procedures is essential. If a lawyer uses third-party electronic or Internet-based file storage, the lawyer must make reasonable efforts to ensure that the company has in place, or will establish reasonable procedures to protect the confidentiality of client information. See, ABA Formal Ethics Opinion 398 (1995). Records required by Rule 1 shall be readily accessible and shall be readily available to be produced upon request by the client or third person who has an interest as provided in Model Rule 1.15, or by the official request of a disciplinary authority, including but not limited to, a subpoena duces tecum. Personally identifying information in records produced upon request by the client or third person or by disciplinary authority shall remain confidential and shall be disclosed only in a manner to ensure client confidentiality as otherwise required by law or court rule.

[2] Rule 28 of the Model Rules for Lawyer Disciplinary Enforcement provides for the preservation of a lawyer's client trust account records in the event that the lawyer is transferred to disability inactive status, suspended, disbarred, disappears, or dies.

RULE 4: DISSOLUTION OF LAW FIRM

Upon dissolution of a law firm or of any legal professional corporation, the partners shall make reasonable arrangements for the maintenance of client trust account records specified in Rule 1.

Comment

[1] Rules 4 and 5 provide for the preservation of a lawyer's client trust account records in the event of dissolution or sale of a law practice. Regardless of the arrangements the partners or shareholders make among themselves for maintenance of the client trust records, each partner may be held responsible for ensuring the availability of these records. For the purposes of these Rules, the terms "law firm," "partner," and "reasonable" are defined in accordance with Rules 1.0(c), (g), and (h) of the Model Rules of Professional Conduct

RULE 5: SALE OF LAW PRACTICE

Upon the sale of a law practice, the seller shall make reasonable arrangements for the maintenance of records specified in Rule 1.

Appendix G

Recap of Selected ABA Model Rules of Professional Conduct

The following rules are offered as guidelines; states may have modified them, adopted them in part, adopted them with additions, or simply adopted their own rules. Know which rules apply in your state.

Model Rules 1.1, 1.3, and 1.4 require that a lawyer exercise competence and diligence in handling client matters, keep the client reasonably informed of the status of the client's case, and comply with a client's reasonable request for information. The paralegal can help the lawyer comply with these rules by the timely completion of assignments and by making certain that clients receive appropriate copies of correspondence and documents related to their matter. The paralegal should ask the lawyer to establish a policy regarding which items of information may be routinely sent to the client and which need specific authorization from the lawyer. Paralegals also may draft status letters for the lawyer's signature or approval and work to formulate a system for timely response to telephone calls and correspondence.

Model Rule 1.5 relates to the lawyer's fee and the obligation to advise the client promptly of the rate that will be charged. It also discusses contingent fees and fee division. Paralegals may prepare representation agreements in the form approved by the lawyer for the lawyer's signature and presentation to the client. A written fee agreement provides proper information for billing purposes.

Model Rule 1.6 prohibits disclosure of information concerning representation of a client, subject to certain exceptions. For example, a lawyer may reveal information necessary to prevent a client from taking action that would result in someone's reasonably certain death or substantial bodily harm. Sometimes clients divulge only to the paralegal their intent to inflict injury on others. The paralegal should report such statements to the lawyer immediately. It would be prudent for the lawyer to discuss with the paralegal exactly what action, if any, should be taken if the lawyer is unavailable and the client's ability to carry out the threat is real and imminent.

Model Rules 1.7, 1.8, 1.9, and 1.10 relate to conflicts of interest. As a general proposition, loyalty to a client prohibits undertaking representation directly adverse to that client without that client's consent. Lawyers consider whether the representation in question will materially interfere with the lawyer's independent professional judgment in handling the client's case. Paralegals have access to material information relating to the representation of clients. Exposure to facts, legal analysis, and lawyer strategies mandates that potential conflicts of interest that can be applied to a lawyer also can be applied to a paralegal. Ultimately, the confidences and secrets of clients must be preserved, and paralegals are charged with the duty to inform employers of any potential conflict of interest.

Model Rule 1.14 discusses obligations due a client with diminished capacity. It provides that the lawyer shall, as far as reasonably possible, maintain a normal client-lawyer relationship. Clients with diminished capacities may impose additional responsibilities on the lawyer; however, the lawyer still has an obligation to obtain information from the client to the extent possible. A lawyer may seek the appointment of a guardian or take other protective action with respect to a client only when the lawyer reasonably believes that the client cannot act in the client's own interest. Paralegals may be involved in gathering information from a client with diminished capacity. The client's diminished capacity does not relieve paralegals of the responsibility and obligation to treat the client with attention, respect, and objectivity.

Model Rule 1.15 relates to safekeeping of property and enumerates the lawyer's responsibility with regard to trust accounts or other property. Maintaining client trust account records is often delegated to the paralegal. Paralegals should regard it as a grave responsibility and give it the highest priority. Paralegals must be absolutely certain they understand the obligations and constraints imposed with regard to such accounts in a specific state and follow them meticulously. Improper accounting or maintenance of client trust accounts often results in harsh sanctions against the lawyer. It is not unusual for a lawyer to be disbarred for irregularities in his or her trust account, regardless of how they occurred, who was responsible, or the amount involved.

Model Rule 1.18 deals with duties to prospective clients. When a lawyer discusses the possibility of forming a client-lawyer relationship with someone, confidentiality and conflicts considerations attach. The paralegal who is given information regarding the prospective client from the lawyer or from the prospective client must be careful to treat that information in the same confidential manner as if it had been received from a client.

Model Rule 3.1 relates to meritorious claims and contentions. While the lawyer in the advocate role has the duty to use legal procedure to the fullest benefit of the client, there is also a duty not to abuse the law. In a paralegal's support of the lawyer through factual and legal research to develop the client's claim, the paralegal should be certain to provide the lawyer with complete and current facts and relevant legal authority, both in support of and in opposition to the claim advanced. The lawyer then can assess properly the client's claim and the position to be taken.

Model Rule 3.2 imposes the obligation on the lawyer to make reasonable efforts to expedite litigation. A paralegal's timely completion of delegated assignments will help avoid delays in litigation matters.

Model Rule 3.3 relates to the advocate's duty of candor to the tribunal. This rule includes prohibitions against the lawyer making false statements and offering evidence known to be false. It also provides that the lawyer must reveal any adverse authority known to the lawyer to the tribunal. A paralegal's conduct must comport with that required of the lawyer. The paralegal may not engage in creating or advancing any false statements or false evidence.

Model Rule 3.4 relates to fairness to opposing parties and counsel. This rule prohibits obstruction of access to evidence and the alteration, destruction, or concealment of documents or material of potential evidentiary value. Falsifying evidence or assisting a witness to testify falsely is also prohibited. The lawyer may not circumvent this rule by having a paralegal engage in the prohibited conduct.

Model Rule 3.5 prohibits a lawyer from seeking to influence a judge, juror, prospective juror, or other official; communicating ex parte with such persons except as permitted by law; and engaging in conduct intended to disrupt a tribunal. A paralegal should not discuss the case with the judge, juror, or other proscribed party unless authorized to do so.

Model Rule 3.6 relates to trial publicity and extrajudicial statements by the lawyer concerning proceedings. A paralegal should not make any statements to the media that would jeopardize a client's right of privacy.

Model Rule 3.7 sets forth the parameters for the lawyer acting as both an advocate and a witness in the proceeding. Although a paralegal will not be acting as a direct advocate, if he or she is a potential witness in a case, the concerns are similar to those of a lawyer/witness. The paralegal should make that fact known to the lawyer who will then assess the appropriate role for the paralegal in the particular case.

Model Rule 3.9 relates to the lawyer acting as an advocate before a legislative or administrative body in a non-adjudicative proceeding. This rule requires that the lawyer appearing before such a body deal with the tribunal honestly and in conformity with the applicable rules of procedure. A paralegal may be allowed to take a direct role as an advocate in some administrative proceedings. If the rules and regulations provide that a paralegal may appear on behalf of a client before such a body, the paralegal's conduct should conform to that imposed on the lawyer and to any rules and regulations promulgated by the administrative agency.

Model Rule 4.1 requires truthfulness in statements to others. A paralegal should always clearly identify his or her status as a paralegal in the work setting. A paralegal should make certain that the lawyer identifies the paralegal's status to opposing counsel and to the judge.

Model Rule 4.2 prohibits direct communications by lawyers with persons and opposing parties represented by other lawyers. A paralegal may not engage in such contact to circumvent that prohibition.

Model Rule 4.3 prohibits a lawyer from misleading an unrepresented person about the lawyer's role in a matter.

Model Rule 5.3 provides that a lawyer must educate the paralegal regarding his or her ethical obligations. The paralegal must be familiar with all rules governing the professional responsibilities of lawyers in the jurisdiction in which they practice. This will include familiarity with applicable ethics opinions and decisions.

Model Rule 5.5 prohibits a lawyer from assisting a person who is not a member of the bar in the performance of activity that constitutes the unauthorized practice of law. The definition of the practice of law varies from one jurisdiction to another. Whatever the definition, the practice of law is limited to members of the bar. Lawyers may delegate functions to paralegals as long as the lawyer supervises the delegated work and retains responsibility for it. This rule also deals with multijurisdictional practice. A paralegal who works for a lawyer who provides services in states other than the one in which the lawyer is licensed should be familiar with these new provisions.

Model Rule 6.1 recommends that lawyers aspire to provide at least 50 hours of pro bono publico legal services per year. Every lawyer has an ethical responsibility to provide legal services to those unable to pay. There are numerous opportunities for paralegals to do pro bono work. Paralegals must inform clients that they are not lawyers. Lawyer supervision is required for all legal services performed for the client.

Model Rules 7.1, 7.2, 7.3, 7.4, and 7.5 govern communications about a lawyer's services, including advertising. While the rules are most often implicated in the context of legal advertising, they are not limited to advertisements and apply to any communication by a lawyer. The underpinning of the rules is that a lawyer should not make false or misleading statements about the lawyer or the lawyer's services. With a proper understanding of these rules, a paralegal can play an important role in marketing the law firm's services and ensuring that those marketing activities are conducted in an ethical manner.

Model Rule 8.4 prohibits a lawyer from engaging in conduct that involves dishonesty, fraud, deceit or misrepresentation and also from committing misconduct through the acts of another.

The complete ABA Model Rules of Professional Conduct can be ordered through the ABA Service Center, (800) 285-2221, or online at http://shop.americanbar.org. Also available are the Annotated Model Rules of Professional Conduct, Eighth Edition and the ABA Compendium of Professional Responsibility Rules and Standards.

Appendix H

Glossary

AAfPE American Association for Paralegal Education; an association formed for legal assistant educators and institutions that educate legal assistants.

ABA American Bar Association; voluntary national association for lawyers.

Admonition also known as private reprimand, a form of nonpublic discipline that declares the conduct of the lawyer improper but does not limit the lawyer's right to practice law.

Agent one who acts on behalf of a principal who is ultimately responsible for the work performed by the subordinate within the scope of employment. The agent is subject to the principal's control; thus, the legal assistant, acting as the agent of a lawyer, is subject to the lawyer's direction.

Aspirational Standards objectives toward which every member of the legal profession should strive; a violation of these standards does not result in disciplinary action.

Attorney-Client Privilege a rule of evidence protecting communications between a lawyer and a client from disclosure.

Civil Liability Responsibility under civil law to pay monetary damages or otherwise make amends for one's actions that have harmed another.

Client Protection Funds programs established under the supervision of the highest court of a jurisdiction to reimburse clients who have lost money or property as a result of a lawyer's dishonest conduct.

Competence the legal knowledge, skill, thoroughness, and preparation reasonably necessary for the representation of a client.

Complainant a person who files a disciplinary complaint against a lawyer.

Confidentiality the basic ethical principle that any information a client entrusts to a lawyer shall not be disclosed by the lawyer unless disclosure is authorized, necessary to the representation of the client, or the client gives informed consent to disclosure.

Conflict of Interest a situation that interferes with a lawyer's ability to fulfill basic duties of candor, confidentiality, and loyalty to a client; conflicts may arise due to a lawyer's own personal interests in a matter, another existing client's interests, or a former client's interests.

Continuing Legal Education (CLE) educational courses offered to members of the bar; some jurisdictions mandate courses and credit hours per year (mandatory continuing legal education); in other jurisdictions CLE is voluntary.

Costs out-of-pocket expenses incurred in bringing a legal action, such as filing fees.

Court-Appointed Counsel a lawyer appointed by the court to represent a person who cannot afford to hire a lawyer.

Disbarment revocation of a lawyer's license to practice law because of the lawyer's breach of professional conduct rules; usually for a period of at least five years, in some jurisdictions disbarment is permanent.

Disciplinary Counsel a lawyer appointed by the highest court of a jurisdiction to investigate and prosecute allegations of professional misconduct by lawyers.

Disclosure informing the client or former client of the relevant circumstances and the actual and reasonably foreseeable adverse consequences to the client or former client.

Document Preparer a person who assists in the preparation of forms and documents; a copyist who usually types in commercially produced and court-approved forms but may also use word processing computers to produce computer-generated forms; provides no advice such as which forms to choose or how to answer questions on the forms.

Ethical Wall (or Screen) an office procedure for preventing a law firm from being disqualified from representing a client because one of the firm's lawyers possesses confidential information obtained from that lawyer's representation of the client's adversary while the lawyer was in government service or employed by another law firm. To be effective, the lawyer possessing the confidential information should not participate in the matter, should not discuss the matter with any member of the firm, should represent that no confidential information has been imparted to the firm, should not have access to any files or documents related to the matter, and should not share any of the fees from the matter.

Ethics Advisory Opinion an opinion issued by a bar association or other legal organization that applies professional conduct rules to specific factual situations; the opinion offers guidance but is not legally binding.

Ex Parte Communication a communication between a lawyer or party and a judicial officer about a case outside the presence of the opposing lawyer or party in the matter.

Fiduciary Duty a lawyer's duty to act for someone else's benefit, while subordinating the lawyer's personal interests to that of the other person.

Fitness to Practice Law the capacity to conduct the practice of law without moral, ethical, or personal impediments.

Indigent a client who is unable to afford legal services.

Informed Consent a client's or former client's decision to accept or allow representation following disclosure by the lawyer of any possible adverse interests; both the lawyer's disclosure and the client's consent should be in writing.

Interest on Lawyers Trust Accounts (IOLTA) interest earned from pooled client funds that is accrued and used in various approved activities to further the administration of justice.

Interim Suspension the temporary removal of a lawyer from the practice of law when there is sufficient evidence to show that the lawyer has committed a violation of the rules of professional conduct or is under a disability and poses a substantial threat of serious harm to the public.

IPMA International Practice Management Association; an association for paralegals in managerial positions.

Law Office Management managing the administrative and financial aspects of a law practice through a set of specially designed systems such as conflict of interest screens, billing and bookkeeping procedures, and information access protection.

Lay Representation appearance by a nonlawyer before an agency or other tribunal on behalf of another without the direct supervision of a lawyer.

Legal Malpractice Insurance insurance coverage carried by lawyers that offers monetary protection to clients in the event of professional malpractice.

Malpractice a legal action that may result when a lawyer is professionally negligent or breaches a professional duty owed to a client or, in limited situations, a third party. There must be damage to the client or third party's interests and a showing that the damage would not have occurred but for the lawyer's conduct, the propriety of which is measured against the expected norm in such situations. Unlike an ethical breach, malpractice is a civil matter pursued in the civil court system.

Misappropriation any unauthorized use of a client's funds or property entrusted to a lawyer, including not only theft but also unauthorized temporary use for the lawyer's own purpose, whether or not the lawyer derives any personal gain or benefit.

Motion for Disqualification a trial procedure whereby a lawyer or law firm is sought to be removed from representing a party because of an alleged conflict of interest.

Multistate Practice providing legal services in two or more jurisdictions.

NALA National Association of Legal Assistants; a voluntary national association for paralegals.

NFPA National Federation of Paralegal Associations; a voluntary national association of paralegal organizations.

Officer of the Court a title for lawyers acknowledging them as members of the legal system with an obligation to ensure the administration of justice; as an officer of the court, a lawyer owes a duty of candor to the court, among other duties.

Paralegal a person, qualified through education, training, or work experience, who is employed or retained by a lawyer, law office, governmental agency, or other entity in a capacity or function that involves the performance, under the ultimate direction and supervision of a lawyer, of specifically delegated substantive legal work, which, for the most part, requires a sufficient knowledge of legal concepts that, absent such assistant, the lawyer would perform.

Perjury testifying falsely under oath to a court, either in a deposition or affidavit, or from the witness stand.

Probation a sanction that allows a lawyer to practice law under specified conditions.

Pro Bono Publico a Latin phrase meaning "for the public good"; refers to legal work undertaken without the expectation of being paid.

Professionalism conducting oneself according to the highest values of the legal profession, with a spirit of public service.

Pro Se a Latin term meaning to represent oneself in court without a lawyer.

Prosecutorial Misconduct when a state or federal prosecutor breaches the special obligations of his or her office.

Puffery exaggerating one's skills or abilities in public communications to encourage members of the public to retain the lawyer's services.

Reciprocal Discipline the imposition of a disciplinary sanction by a jurisdiction for conduct for which a lawyer previously has been disciplined in another jurisdiction.

Recusal a judge's decision to not hear a case because of a possible inability or appearance of inability to render an impartial judgment.

Reinstatement reestablishing a lawyer's license to practice law after a lawyer has fulfilled the requirements of a disciplinary order.

Reprimand a form of discipline that declares the conduct of the lawyer improper but does not limit the lawyer's right to practice.

Respondent a lawyer who is subject to a disciplinary complaint.

Respondent's Counsel a lawyer who represents another lawyer in a disciplinary proceeding.

Restitution an order to repay a party that has been injured due to a lawyer's breach of the professional conduct rules.

Sanction the discipline imposed upon a lawyer who violates the rules of professional conduct.

Screening (1) an office procedure for ensuring that a law firm does not take on conflicting representations; (2) a procedure for isolating a "tainted" lawyer or legal assistant who would otherwise disqualify a law firm from a representation because of access to confidential information. (See also Ethical Wall.)

Solicitation the attempt to gain legal business by offering legal services directly to potential clients, either in person, by targeted written communication, or by live telephone contact; does not apply to offers of legal services without charge.

Suspension the removal of a lawyer from the practice of law for a specified minimum period of time.

Unauthorized Practice of Law nonlawyer, or suspended or disbarred lawyer, engaging in the practice of law, such as representing clients, setting legal fees, drafting legal documents, or giving legal advice without a law license; parameters vary from one jurisdiction to another.

Unified Bar state bar association where lawyers are required to become members of the association.

Voluntary Bar state bar association where lawyers may choose to become members of the association.

Waiver surrendering a legal right to which one is otherwise entitled.

Work Product Doctrine an evidentiary rule extending the protection of the attorney-client privilege to work product of a lawyer containing or revealing the lawyer's mental impressions about a client's case (e.g., interoffice memos). The work product doctrine may encompass a wider scope of materials than the attorney-client privilege, but the attorney-client privilege is absolute and therefore stronger than the work product privilege, which is a "qualified" privilege.

Index

ABA. *See* American Bar Association
Administrative proceedings, representation in, 41, 45
Advertising regulations, 15, 105–110, 113–115
Agents, paralegals as, 2–3, 4, 12, 26
Alabama, code of ethics in, 26
American Association for Paralegal Education (AAfPE), 7, 55
American Bar Association (ABA)
  Canons of Professional Ethics, 26
  Center for Professional Responsibility, 48n19, 107
  Commission on Lawyer Assistance Programs, 32, 57, 60
  Commission on Nonlawyer Practice, 44–46
  Commission on Professionalism (Stanley Commission), 7
  contact information for, 6
  education and training support/criteria by, 5–6, 56
  ethics opinions by, 28, 77, 86, 114
  Guidelines for the Approval of Paralegal Education Programs, 6
  House of Delegates, 5–6, 58, 134
  Model Guidelines for the Utilization of Paralegal Services, 13, 16–17, 29, 85
  Model Law Firm/Legal Department Personnel Impairment Policy and Guidelines, 58
  Model Rule for Payee Notification, 136
  Model Rule for Random Audit of Trust Accounts, 140–141
  Model Rule for Trust Account Overdraft Notification, 136
  Model Rules for Client Trust Account Records, 134–135
  Model Rules for Fee Arbitration, 124
  Model Rules of Professional Conduct, 2, 12–13, 18, 22n8, 26–28, 32, 38, 42, 49–57, 66, 69–73, 75–76, 82–92, 97–102, 108–112, 120–122, 125, 130, 131–138
  paralegal profession support through, 5–6
  Standing Committee on Client Protection, 48n19, 124
  Standing Committee on Ethics and Professional Responsibility, 72–73
  Standing Committee on Paralegals, 4, 5–6
Arizona, laws of professional responsibility in, 25

Attorney-client privilege, 63, 64–65, 66–67, 75, 76. See also Confidentiality
Attorneys. See Lawyers
Audits, 140–141

Barratry statutes, 112
Barrett, State v. (1971), 21n5
Bates v. State Bar of Arizona (1977), 106
Billing and collection, 121–125
Bookkeeping, 15–17, 20, 132–134. See also Client funds and property
Business cards, 110–111

California, laws of professional responsibility in, 25, 27
Case managers, 42–43
Certified Paralegal exam, 55, 56
Civil proceedings, representation in, 41
Client funds and property
 adequate bookkeeping for, 132–134
 advance payments as, 125, 134
 disputes about, 138–139
 financial records of, 134–135, 136–137
 Interest on Lawyer Trust Accounts on, 125, 139
 lawyers' fund for client protection of, 140
 legal services delivery team handling of, 15–17, 20, 21n3, 21n5
 Model Rules of Professional Conduct on, 130, 131–138
 overview of, 129, 141
 paralegal's safekeeping of, 129–130
 proper notification on, 135–138
 random audits of trust accounts for, 140–141
 segregation of, 131–134, 138

Clients
 communication with, 44, 97
 confidentiality related to, 17, 63–79, 88–92
 conflicts of interest related to, 17, 66–67, 81–96
 corporations as, 42, 70
 current vs. former, 84
 funds and property of, 15–17, 20, 21n3, 21n5, 125, 129–143
 gifts from, 87–88
 identity of, 68
 legal advice to, 39–40
 legal fees charged to, 1–2, 17, 53, 69, 85–86, 108, 119–127, 134
 legal services providers for (see Lawyers; Legal services delivery team; Paralegals)
 multiple, in same or related matter, 77
 perjury by, 72–73
 representation in court and other proceedings for, 40–42, 43, 45, 66–67, 72, 73, 82–83
 sexual relations with, 87
 solicitation of, 111–112
Communications
 with clients, 44, 97
 correspondence as, 4, 44, 51
 false or misleading, prohibition of, 107–110
 with judges, 98
 with jurors/prospective jurors, 98–99
 in legal services delivery team, 11, 14
 overview of, 103
 with person represented by council, 100–101
 public, 102
 truthfulness of, 102, 107–110

Index

with unrepresented persons, 101–102
Compensation, paralegal, 1–2, 17, 122–123, 126. *See also* Legal fees
Competence and diligence
  education and training for, 55–57
  knowledge and skill in, 50–52
  in legal research, 51, 52–53
  Model Rules of Professional Conduct on, 49–57
  overview of, 49, 60
  substance abuse impacting, 57–60
  testing for, 55–56
  thoroughness and preparation in, 52
Confidentiality
  attorney-client privilege rule of, 63, 64–65, 66–67, 75, 76
  authorized and unauthorized disclosures of, 70–73
  changes of employment and issues of, 72, 88–92
  claim establishment or self-defense, breach allowances for, 72
  client perjury, breach allowances for, 72–73
  conflicts of interest related to, 66–67, 88–92
  of corporation representatives, 70
  of criminal evidence, 69
  discovery request fulfillment within, 74–75
  discussing client matters as breach of, 73–74
  ethical rule of, 63–64, 65–66, 72, 75, 77
  of identity, 68
  inadvertent disclosure of confidential information, 65, 75, 76
  of information relating to representation, 66–67, 72

of legal fees, 69
Model Guidelines for the Utilization of Paralegal Services on, 17
Model Rules of Professional Conduct on, 66, 69–73, 75–76
of multiple clients in same or related matters, 77
office maintenance and sharing issues of, 67–68, 74
overview of, 63–64, 77
paralegal-specific issues with, 64–65, 73–77
past acts rectification, breach allowances for, 71
prevention of bodily harm, crime, or fraud, breach allowances for, 70–71, 73
principles of, 63–79
receipt of inadvertent disclosures and, 76
screening measures to maintain, 65, 67, 89–92
sharing confidences in the workplace within, 67–68
technology use considerations of, 75–76
types of confidential information, 68–69
waiver of, 65
withdrawal of representation and, 73
work product doctrine rule of, 65
Conflicts of interest
  checking system for, 92–93
  confidentiality issues related to, 66–67, 88–92
  current vs. former clients as, 84
  directly adverse representation as, 82–83
  duty to avoid, 81–96
  general considerations with, 82

gifts from clients as, 87–88
interest in the litigation as, 85–86
issue conflicts as, 83
lawyers and paralegals switching firms as, 88–92
lawyer's own interests as, 84–85
Model Guidelines for the Utilization of Paralegal Services on, 17
Model Rules of Professional Conduct on, 82–92
non-litigation conflicts as, 84
overview of, 81–82, 93
personal relationships as, 86–87
screening measures to avoid, 89–92
sexual relations with clients as, 87
Corporations, 42, 70
Court, legal representation in, 40–42
Criminal evidence, confidentiality of, 69

Deadlines, meeting, 54
Depositions, 4, 43
Disbarment, of lawyers, 15, 28

Education and training
 Certified Paralegal exam in, 55, 56
 Model Guidelines for the Utilization of Paralegal Services on, 17
 NALA membership criteria for, 56–57
 Paralegal Advanced Competency exam in, 55–56
 Paralegal CORE Competency exam in, 55
 of paralegals, 3, 5–6, 7, 12, 13, 14, 17, 51, 55–57
 professional association support for, 5–6, 7, 56–57
 testing for competence in, 55–56

Employment
 compensation for, 1–2, 17, 122–123, 126 (see also Legal fees)
 confidentiality and changes of, 72, 88–92
 principle employers of paralegals, 3
 termination of, for misconduct, 29
Ethics
 codes of ethics, 25–26, 32, 38, 51, 64, 65, 87, 120, 121, 130
 confidentiality, ethical rule of, 63–64, 65–66, 72, 75, 77
 creating an ethical culture, 14
 ethics opinions, 28, 75, 77, 86, 99, 110–111, 114
 misconduct and breach of, 29–32
 rules on professional and ethical conduct (see Law of professional responsibility; Model Rules of Professional Conduct)

Fair Debt Collection Practices Act, 44
Federal agency proceedings, representation in, 41
Fees, legal. *See* Legal fees
Financial issues. *See* Bookkeeping; Client funds and property; Legal fees
Florida
 client funds and property in, 129
 conflicts of interest in, 88
 Registered Paralegals in, 8n2
Funds. *See* Client funds and property

Georgia, legal fees in, 126
Gifts from clients, 87–88
Grubbs, In re (1983), 138–139
Guidelines for the Approval of Paralegal Education Programs (ABA), 6

Himmel, In re (1988), 34–35n14

Identity, confidentiality of, 68
In the Spirit of Public Service: A Blueprint for the Rekindling of Lawyer Professionalism (ABA), 7
Information on legal services
  advertising regulations on, 15, 105–110, 113–115
  Internet-based, 114–115
  limits on firm names and firm letterhead use for, 110–111
  limits on solicitation of clients offering, 111–112
  marketing regulations on, 113–114
  Model Rules of Professional Conduct on, 108–112
  overview of, 105–106, 115
  prohibition of false or misleading communications on, 107–110
  state rules on, 105–106, 107–108, 110–111, 112–115
Interest on Lawyer Trust Accounts (IOLTA), 125, 139
International Practice Management Association (IPMA), 7
Internet-based technology, 51, 75, 98–99, 101, 102, 114–115

Kansas, conflicts of interest in, 88
Kentucky, unauthorized practice of law in, 43

Law of professional responsibility
  consequences of misconduct under, 29–30
  ethics opinions on, 28
  evolution of rules of professional conduct for, 26–27
  local rules as, 27–28
  model codes of ethics reflecting, 25–26, 32
  Model Guidelines for the Utilization of Paralegal Services informing, 29
  overview of, 32–33
  reporting of misconduct under, 31–32, 34–35n14
  rules for paralegals under, 25–26
  sanctions for breaking, 28–29
Lawyers
  agents of, 2–3, 4, 12, 26
  attorney-client privilege for, 63, 64–65, 66–67, 75, 76 (*see also* Confidentiality)
  changes of employment by, 72, 88–92
  clients of (*see* Clients)
  communications by/with, 4, 11, 14, 44, 51, 97–104, 107–110
  conflicts of interest for, 17, 66–67, 81–96
  creating an ethical culture by, 14 (*see also* Ethics)
  disbarment of, 15, 28
  information on legal services rules for, 15, 105–118
  law of professional responsibility for, 25–35
  legal advice from, 39–40
  legal fees charged by, 1–2, 17, 53, 69, 85–86, 108, 119–127, 134
  legal services delivery team including, 11–23
  license of, to practice law, 37, 38
  office procedures, maintenance, and sharing of, 14–17, 67–68, 74
  paralegals' relationship with, 1–3 (*see also* Agents, paralegals as; Supervision of paralegals)
  professionalism of, 7–8

representation by, 40–42, 43, 45, 66–67, 72, 73, 82–83
substance abuse issues among, 32, 57–60
successor to, 54
supervision of paralegals by, 11–20, 22n8, 38, 42
Legal advice, 39–40
Legal documents, 42, 51, 65
Legal fees
 advance payments for, 124–125, 134
 billing and collection of, 121–125
 confidentiality of fee information, 69
 contingent, 85–86, 108, 121
 contract labor in, 123–124
 fee agreements on, 120–121, 123
 for legal research, 53
 Model Guidelines for the Utilization of Paralegal Services on, 17
 Model Rules of Professional Conduct on, 120–122, 125
 overview of, 119–120, 126
 paralegal compensation and, 1–2, 17, 122–123, 126
 paralegal's role in, 119–127
 reasonableness of, 122, 124
 retainers for, 124
 sharing of, 125–126
Legal research, 4, 51, 52–53
Legal services, information on. *See* Information on legal services
Legal services delivery team. *See also* Lawyers; Paralegals
 client funds and property handled by, 15–17, 20, 21n3, 21n5
 communication in, 11, 14
 creating an ethical culture for, 14
 education and training for, 12, 13, 14, 17

Model Guidelines for the Utilization of Paralegal Services for, 13, 16–17
 office procedures for, 14–17
 overview of, 11, 20–21
 paralegals in, 11–23
 specific prohibitions and concerns for, 19–20
 substantive assignments to, 18–19
 supervision of paralegals in, 11–20, 22n8
 unauthorized practice of law by, 16, 18
Letterhead, firm, 110–111
Licensure
 for paralegals, 3, 33n1
 to practice law, 37, 38
Local rules, 27–28. *See also* States

Marketing regulations, 113–114
Misconduct
 client funds and property mishandling as, 137–138, 139, 140
 consequences of, 29–30
 non-truthful communications as, 102
 reporting of, 31–32, 34–35n14
Misrepresentation of status, 43–44
Missouri v. Jenkins (1989), 4
Model Guidelines for the Utilization of Paralegal Services (ABA), 13, 16–17, 29, 85
Model Law Firm/Legal Department Personnel Impairment Policy and Guidelines (ABA), 58
Model Rule for Payee Notification (ABA), 136
Model Rule for Random Audit of Trust Accounts (ABA), 140–141
Model Rule for Trust Account Overdraft Notification (ABA), 136

Model Rules for Client Trust Account
    Records (ABA), 134–135
Model Rules for Fee Arbitration
    (ABA), 124
Model Rules of Professional Conduct
    (ABA)
  on agent misconduct, 2
  on client funds and property, 130,
    131–138
  on communications, 97–102
  on competence and diligence,
    49–57
  on confidentiality, 66, 69–73, 75–76
  on conflicts of interest, 82–92
  on delegation of legal work, 13
  evolution of, 26–27
  on information on legal services,
    108–112
  on knowledge, 32
  on legal fees, 120–122, 125
  local rules based on, 27–28
  on supervision of paralegals,
    12–13, 22n8, 42
  on unauthorized practice of law,
    18, 27, 38

Names, firm, 110–111
National Association for Legal
    Assistants (NALA)
  code of ethics of, 25–26, 38, 51,
    65, 87, 120
  on confidentiality, 65
  on conflicts of interest, 87
  contact information for, 6
  on definition of paralegal/legal
    assistant, 4
  educational criteria for membership
    in, 56–57
  on legal fees, 120
  on paralegal competence and
    diligence, 51, 55, 56–57

paralegal participation in, 6
  on unauthorized practice of law, 38
National Federation of Paralegal
    Associations (NFPA)
  on client funds and property, 130
  on confidentiality, 64
  contact information for, 6
  on definition of paralegal/legal
    assistant, 4
  on educational requirements, 57
  on legal fees, 121
  model code of ethics of, 25–26, 32,
    38, 51, 64, 121, 130
  on paralegal competence and
    diligence, 51, 55–56
  paralegal participation in, 6
  on unauthorized practice of law, 38
New Jersey, confidentiality in, 71
New Mexico, laws of professional
    responsibility in, 25
New York, unauthorized practice of
    law in, 43
North Carolina, confidentiality in,
    75–76

Office procedures, maintenance, and
    sharing, 14–17, 67–68, 74
Ohio, information on legal services in,
    114–115
Ontario, paralegals in, 33n1
Oregon, unauthorized practice of law
    in, 43

Paralegals
  ABA support for, 5–6
  agency of, 2–3, 4, 12, 26
  client funds and property
    responsibilities of, 15–17, 20,
    21n3, 21n5, 125, 129–143
  communications by/with, 4, 11,
    14, 44, 51, 97–104, 107–110

competence and diligence of, 49–62
confidentiality principles for, 17, 63–79, 88–92
conflicts of interest for, 17, 66–67, 81–96
definition and description of, 3–4
education and training of, 3, 5–6, 7, 12, 13, 14, 17, 51, 55–57
employment of, 1–2, 3, 17, 29, 72, 88–92, 122–123, 126
growth of paralegal profession, 5
information on legal services rules for, 15, 105–118
law of professional responsibility for, 25–35
lawyers' relationship with, 1–3 (see also Agents, paralegals as; Supervision of paralegals)
legal fees and compensation for, 1–2, 17, 53, 69, 85–86, 108, 119–127, 134
legal research by, 4, 51, 52–53
legal services delivery team including, 11–23
licensure for, 3, 33n1
professional associations for, 5–7 (see also specific associations)
professionalism of, 7–8
role of, 1–9, 44–46
substance abuse issues impacting, 32, 57–60
supervision of, 7, 11–20, 22n8, 38, 42
unauthorized practice of law by, 16, 18, 27, 37–48
Pennsylvania, unauthorized practice of law in, 43
Perjury, 72–73
Pound, Roscoe, 7
Privilege, 63, 64–65, 66–67, 75, 76. See also Confidentiality

Professional associations, 5–7. See also specific associations
Professional conduct, rules on. See Law of professional responsibility; Model Rules of Professional Conduct
Professionalism of paralegals, 7–8
Property. See Client funds and property
Public communications, 102

Real estate closings, representation at, 43
Registered Paralegals, 8n2
Representation
 in administrative proceedings, 41, 45
 in civil proceedings, 41
 confidentiality of information related to, 66–67, 72
 of corporations, 42
 in court, 40–42
 directly adverse, 82–83
 in federal agency proceedings, 41
 misrepresentation of status, 43–44
 at real estate closings, 43
 self-representation, 41–42
 withdrawal from, 73
Retainers, 124

Sanctions, 28–29
Scanlan, In re (1985), 21n3
Screening measures, 65, 67, 89–92
Self-representation, 41–42
Sexual relations with clients, 87
Social media, 99, 101, 102
Solicitation of clients, 111–112
South Carolina
 confidentiality in, 71
 unauthorized practice of law in, 43
States. See also Local rules; specific states

barratry statutes in, 112
client funds and property in, 129, 133, 135, 139–140
code of ethics for lawyers in, 26
communications rules in, 99
confidentiality in, 71, 75–76
conflicts of interest in, 88
ethics opinions by, 28, 99, 110–111, 114
guidelines for utilization of paralegal services by, 13, 19
information on legal services in, 105–106, 107–108, 110–111, 112–115
laws of professional responsibility in, 25–26, 27–28
lawyer assistance programs in, 57
legal fees in, 121, 124, 126
unauthorized practice of law in, 43, 45, 48n19
Substance abuse issues, 32, 57–60
Successor lawyers, 54
Supervision of paralegals, 7, 11–20, 22n8, 38, 42

Technology
  communications via, 98–99, 101, 102
  confidentiality issues with, 75–76
  information on legal services via, 114–115
  Internet-based, 51, 75, 98–99, 101, 102, 114–115
  legal research using, 51
  social media via, 99, 101, 102
  websites via, 114
Tennessee, information on legal services in, 114

Unauthorized practice of law
  case managers' actions as, 42–43

codes of ethics on, 38
correspondence signatures creating, 44
deposition attendance as, 43
giving legal advice as, 39–40
law of professional responsibility on, 27
legal document preparation as, 42
misrepresentation of status as, 43–44
Model Guidelines for the Utilization of Paralegal Services on, 16
Model Rules of Professional Conduct on, 18, 27, 38
nonlawyer contributions encouraged mindful of, 44–46
overview of, 46
paralegal's consideration of, 37–38
practice of law by nonlawyers prohibited as, 39–43, 47n2, 47n4
representation in court and other proceedings as, 40–42, 43, 45
state rules on, 43, 45, 48n19
Upjohn Co. v. United States (1981), 70

Virginia, confidentiality in, 71

Washington
  client funds and property in, 139
  laws of professional responsibility in, 25
Websites, 114
Wisconsin, unauthorized practice of law in, 43
Withdrawal from representation, 73
Work product doctrine, 65

barratry statutes in, 112
client funds and property in, 129, 133, 135, 139–140
code of ethics for lawyers in, 26
communications rules in, 99
confidentiality in, 71, 75–76
conflicts of interest in, 88
ethics opinions by, 28, 99, 110–111, 114
guidelines for utilization of paralegal services by, 13, 19
information on legal services in, 105–106, 107–108, 110–111, 112–115
laws of professional responsibility in, 25–26, 27–28
lawyer assistance programs in, 57
legal fees in, 121, 124, 126
unauthorized practice of law in, 43, 45, 48n19
Substance abuse issues, 32, 57–60
Successor lawyers, 54
Supervision of paralegals, 7, 11–20, 22n8, 38, 42

Technology
communications via, 98–99, 101, 102
confidentiality issues with, 75–76
information on legal services via, 114–115
Internet-based, 51, 75, 98–99, 101, 102, 114–115
legal research using, 51
social media via, 99, 101, 102
websites via, 114
Tennessee, information on legal services in, 114

Unauthorized practice of law
case managers' actions as, 42–43

codes of ethics on, 38
correspondence signatures creating, 44
deposition attendance as, 43
giving legal advice as, 39–40
law of professional responsibility on, 27
legal document preparation as, 42
misrepresentation of status as, 43–44
Model Guidelines for the Utilization of Paralegal Services on, 16
Model Rules of Professional Conduct on, 18, 27, 38
nonlawyer contributions encouraged mindful of, 44–46
overview of, 46
paralegal's consideration of, 37–38
practice of law by nonlawyers prohibited as, 39–43, 47n2, 47n4
representation in court and other proceedings as, 40–42, 43, 45
state rules on, 43, 45, 48n19
Upjohn Co. v. United States (1981), 70

Virginia, confidentiality in, 71

Washington
client funds and property in, 139
laws of professional responsibility in, 25
Websites, 114
Wisconsin, unauthorized practice of law in, 43
Withdrawal from representation, 73
Work product doctrine, 65